BEYOND TRUST FALLS

BEYOND TRUST FALLS

The Definitive Guide to Building Teams That Click

DAVID GOLDSTEIN

CEO of TeamBonding

WILEY

Published by John Wiley & Sons, Inc., Hoboken, New Jersey.

For general information on our other products and services or for technical support, please contact our Customer Care Department within the United States at (800) 762-2974, outside the United States at (317) 572-3993 or fax (317) 572-4002.

Wiley also publishes its books in a variety of electronic formats. Some content that appears in print may not be available in electronic formats. For more information about Wiley products, visit our website at www.wiley.com.

Library of Congress Cataloging-in-Publication Data is Available:

ISBN 9781394383184 (Cloth)
ISBN 9781394383191 (ePub)
ISBN 9781394383207 (ePDF)

Cover Design: Jon Boylan
Author Photo: Courtesy of the Author

Printed and bound by CPI Group (UK) Ltd, Croydon, CR0 4YY

C9781394383184_050526

The manufacturer's authorized representative according to the EU General Product Safety Regulation is Wiley-VCH GmbH, Boschstr. 12, 69469 Weinheim, Germany, e-mail: Product_Safety@wiley.com.

For my friend and teammate, Mark Crouthamel.

An entrepreneur in every sense of the word. A creator, a builder, a problem-solver, and the kind of person who dropped everything when help was needed. You fought a brutal battle with courage and grit, never stopping showing up for the people you loved.

Like ice, your work was temporary, but the moments you created were unforgettable, including an ice luge that made Baylee's graduation even more memorable.

A devoted father, grandfather, husband, and friend.
You left your mark on this company, on this book, and on me.
I miss you.

Contents

Introduction

My Journey from Mystery to Team Mastery

They say, "Be nice to people on your way up the ladder . . . because you're going to meet them again on the way down."

I used to think that was just a quaint old expression. Turns out, it's not. I learned that the hard way.

But I'll start from the top and keep this brief.

The Rollercoaster

After graduating from Emerson College with a degree in communication studies in the 1980s, I discovered I had a talent for designing interactive experiences. I started with ski trips and rafting adventures, then moved to unique scavenger hunts, and finally launched America's first murder mystery dinner theater through Comedy Theater Productions and Learning Adventure.

Before I knew it, I had team leaders asking me to run these events for their crews because they were seeing results. The reception blew me away.

By the 1990s, one of our crown jewels was the annual New Year's Eve Extravaganza at the Marriott Long Wharf Hotel in Boston.

Picture this: 500 guests, a live band, champagne flowing, fireworks over the harbor, and a big mystery show. For years, it was *the* event.

And then came the millennium.

The last New Year's Eve party was spectacular, but it marked the end of an era. When 2000 rolled in, the magic had fizzled. Boston was flooded with 37 different dinner theaters, and the roller coaster stopped going up, up, up.

Now it was plummeting and, suddenly, we couldn't pay the bills.

The Decision

The phone started ringing, and every call felt like a punch. Creditors. Demands. Threats. At the office, we called going to work "H-E Double Hockey Sticks" because that's exactly how it felt.

One morning, I'd had enough. I decided I was done. I was going to get a "real job." I sat down at the home computer, scrolling through job listings, trying to figure out my next move.

That's when my daughter Sam, seven years old at the time, wandered in and announced herself by asking, "Daddy, what are you doing?"

She broke through my stress, and I smiled. "I'm looking for a job," I told her.

In my head, I knew exactly what kind of job I wanted. One where I'd go to work in the morning, come home at night, and leave work at the office. No more risks. No more creditors. No more 3 a.m. wake-ups with me wondering how to make payroll.

She frowned at me for a second before asking, "Like Annie's dad?"

"Why? What kind of job does Annie's dad have?"

She looked at me, dead serious. "Well, Annie's dad goes to work in the morning, comes home after she goes to bed, and he never comes to any of her games or events. I don't want you to be like Annie's dad."

Her worried tone stopped me cold.

Right there, I decided that whatever I did next, it had to let me *live* my life, not miss it. That meant figuring out how to make working for myself work again. And so I reassured her that no, I wasn't looking for work "like Annie's dad."

Years later, as I helped my little girl move into her college dorm, I saw Annie and her mom moving in down the hall. But her father? He wasn't there. He was working.

I smiled, remembering that fateful moment and knowing that I'd made the right choice.

The Crossroads

Back in those early days, the morning after Sam and I had our life-changing conversation, I had two paths in front of me: create a team building company combining everything I'd learned, or develop my barhopping tour business.

And listen. . . those bar tours were fun. Late nights, plenty of laughs, questionable decisions.

But I wasn't 25 anymore. I was 37, married, with two kids and another on the way. I wanted to build something sustainable that could bring people together for good reasons. Something that gave me the flexibility to be there for my family.

That's when the spark hit. I realized the most meaningful part of my work wasn't the shows or events themselves—it was how people bonded through them.

The Birth of TeamBonding

I took a hard look at what we had that people loved. The big dinner theaters were done, but smaller private events still had potential. Companies were looking for ways to bring their people together.

Along the way, I found inspiration from unexpected places and partnered with incredibly skilled people who shared my vision. Now I had ideas, energy, and momentum. But I needed a name.

One day, while flipping through something from Disney, I came across "team bonding." It wasn't "team building." It wasn't training. It was something in between—capturing exactly what I wanted to create.

I grabbed the domain TeamBonding.com and started building a brand.

We launched new programs. Custom game shows like Survivor—only in our version, you voted people *onto* the island. Spy School. Partners in Crime. The Original Limousine Scavenger Hunt. Play the Blues, a blues harmonica program where participants learned to play music in an hour. Culinary experiences and cooking competitions.

Slowly, piece by piece, TeamBonding came to life.

When we started, it was the era of trust falls. Team building was seen as a novelty. Over time, though, companies evolved, and so did we.

We grew alongside HR departments as they shifted from policies and paperwork to company culture, employee engagement, and retention. We became part of a bigger story—one where companies understood that their success depended on their people's success.

And for people to succeed, they need to connect. They need to work together, have fun together, and engage in meaningful ways. That's what we built TeamBonding to do.

Why It Still Matters

That period of losing the dinner theaters, facing creditors, and questioning myself was one of the hardest times of my life. But it's also what shaped TeamBonding into what it is today. It taught me resilience. It taught me to listen. And it taught me to reinvent before you're forced to.

Most importantly, it reminded me why I started all of this:

To create work that lets me live my life, spend time with my family, and help other teams connect, create, and grow together.

About This Book

If you've ever wondered why some teams just *click* while others never feel like a team at all, or suffered through painful icebreakers and forced fun, this book is for you. It's not another theoretical business book filled with buzzwords and platitudes. It's a practical guide built from over 35 years of real-world experience, thousands of hours of team building, and the latest neuroscience on how humans actually connect, learn, and grow together.

This is a guide for anyone who believes that people's happiness, connection, and ability to show up as their authentic selves matter just as much as what they do. It's for:

- ♦ **Leaders** who want to inspire rather than instruct, and those trying to connect to a disengaged team to tap into their potential.
- ♦ **Managers and business owners** who want engagement to mean something in their company, and those seeking a real competitive advantage that'll actually stick.
- ♦ **Educators, coaches, and entrepreneurs** who are building their own cultures of connection by bringing people together with authenticity.
- ♦ **Anyone** who knows that a team's strength lies not in its structure, but in its spirit, and those who believe that work should feel and be more human.

You'll find stories, science, and strategies hard-won from decades in the field across multiple professionals and perspectives. You'll find proof that play, done with intention, can transform not just teams, but workplaces, relationships, and even lives.

This book is about team building in its entirety, the countless people who've taught me what real teamwork looks like: facilitators, clients, leaders, and dreamers who've turned play into progress.

An Expert-Guided Journey

While writing this book, I had the pleasure of interviewing several of the most experienced, skilled professionals in this industry to create an expert-guided journey for *you*.

Why?

Because one theme of this book is the power that comes from diverse minds who aren't afraid to share their ideas and insights— that's something team building programs are designed to foster. It's why diversity is so highly valued in some of today's most successful companies.

Insights from a single skilled and experienced person are valuable, but you'll almost always get more from several people putting their heads together. And if those people are all from different cultures, backgrounds, and walks of life, you'll get even more from this meeting of minds because now you have people looking at things from several different angles.

When I started making my list of interviewees, I thought about an old Buddhist parable about blind men and an elephant:

A group of blind men who've never encountered an elephant are asked to describe this animal by touching only one part at a time. One touches the tusks, another the side, another the tail, another the foot, and so on. Then they each describe the elephant based on what they felt. As you'd imagine, each one explains something completely different. But when they combine their experiences into one description, suddenly they have a much clearer picture of what an elephant actually is. It goes from being like a curved spear, a leather wall, a hairy rope, and a tree trunk to being an *elephant*—a complete, complex creature that none of them could fully understand with their individual experience.

One person's perspective will never give you as clear a picture of anything as multiple perspectives will. It's my goal to give you a complete picture of the power of team building, told from multiple angles and experiences, rather than just my personal perspective.

Am I proud of what I've accomplished? Do I feel like I fully understand team building? Am I confident in my ability to design effective programs? Of course I am! But guess what? My time in this industry has also made me a huge believer in the power of teamwork.

What You'll Learn and Who You'll Hear From

Here's a sneak peek of each part of this book and whose perspective(s) they feature:

Introduction: More Than Trust Falls with Julia Holladay

Discover what team building really is (and isn't) and how it has evolved into what it is today. We'll explore why it matters to everyone to find out what you stand to gain from this book.

Part I: The Why Behind the Work with Tyler Hayden

Learn why I focus so much on play and how it changes businesses before we look at the neuroscience behind connection. See why engaged teams are happier and productive and how companies can foster this mindset.

Part II: The Art of Designing Team Moments with Paul Giroux

Discover the ins and outs of how team building professionals assess team needs and prepare to run amazing, impactful events. We'll help you master the framework for designing these events with intention every step of the way.

Part III: The Activities That Move Teams with Shannon Lane DuPont and Jayne Hannah

Get practical, field-tested activities and icebreakers (aka energizers) designed for every team, and find out why charity events are surprisingly effective. You'll also learn several DIY activities for every team type and size, in every setting—whether in-person, remote, or hybrid.

Part IV: Making It Stick with Rob Fletcher

Learn about the final step of making team building effective: the debrief. We discuss the best ways to measure the impact of these events so you can turn them into lasting cultural shifts that drive tangible, trackable results instead of one-offs.

Conclusion: The Future of Teams Is Human with Wendy, Sam, Baylee, and Ty Goldstein

Find out where team building is going, why it's more important now than ever before, and why the human element will always provide the greatest competitive advantage in every industry.

Meet Your First Expert Guide: Julia Holladay

To kick things off, I'm thrilled to introduce you to your first expert guide, Julia Holladay! She's a board-certified coach who specializes in leadership development and personal mastery.

Julia and I go way back. She was TeamBonding's first licensee in California, and during those years, we learned so much from each other and our experience about what makes teams truly click.

These days, Julia spends her time coaching leaders through major career transitions and helping them reconnect with passions they've buried under years of "being professional." She's worked with everyone from nervous young managers looking to prove themselves to seasoned executives who've lost their spark of creativity somewhere along the way. What makes Julia invaluable for this part of the book is her understanding of both the individual psychology of growth *and* the collective dynamics of teams.

She always brings a refreshing honesty to conversations about team building because she's seen the good and the bad—and the painfully awkward trust falls and icebreakers. She knows what makes people cringe and roll their eyes and, more importantly, what actually sparks genuine change.

The Evolution of Team Building: From Entertainment to Essential

When I started TeamBonding, "team building" meant trust falls and unnatural icebreakers—things most people had to endure. Companies saw it as a nice-to-have or, at best, something to check off the corporate culture list.

But something was shifting. Leaders were starting to ask about experiences that went deeper than surface-level trust falls and forced fun. They wanted their teams to learn how to collaborate and communicate better, not just pretend. And they were willing to try unconventional means to get there.

Julia Holladay saw this shift firsthand. "We had leaders realizing how important it is for employees to truly get out of their comfort zone and feel like different people, at least in a small way, after having gone through a profound experience. When that happens, something shifts inside them and something important happens . . . You build memories together, and that changes everything."

We were more than ready for this change in perspective. Our early clients didn't just want to have fun; they wanted to *grow*. Combining growth with fun is how I discovered the real value of play and created conditions where learning, empathy, and trust could take root. People started showing up as themselves, and that told us we could definitely keep up with this shift.

From Forced Activities to Genuine Transformation

Julia explains what actually creates lasting impact:

> "I think today's team building lets you get to know people in a different way, and that translates back into work with more of a connection, more empathy, and more likability. It's nice for everyone when the playing field is leveled enough that the normal hierarchy gets shifted."

This was a fundamental evolution for how I approach team building. You don't want forced participation, predictable outcomes, and fixed roles. No, all of that already happens in most workplaces. Team building needs to mix it up! It has to create environments where the usual power dynamics dissolve, because putting people in situations where no one is the expert leads to something different. And that's what leaders started asking for when things changed.

Julia shares a memorable example from her early days with TeamBonding: "There was a high-end leadership organization, and they had to put on these Johnny Jumpsuits and do crazy art projects. They all had a lot of thoughts about their image going on, and I liked watching this bizarre room full of people with paint everywhere, making art and laughing as they realized, 'Oh, this is all okay, this is fun!'"

That shift from leaders who were protecting their professional images to embracing real vulnerability truly separates modern team building from what it used to be. I think of it as the difference between going through the motions and actually working to improve yourself, which is a whole different beast.

From Optional Perk to Business Imperative

With the changing perception of team building and the evolution of the workplace itself, leaders quit dismissing these activities as a nice, pointless day out of the office that cuts into productivity. Now they recognize how essential they are to organizational success.

"The less automated and the more engaged we can be with each other, the more human we remain and the more compassionate we are," Julia explains. "That human compassion is the biggest advantage we have over AI, which is causing yet another big shift as we speak, and we want to keep that."

And it's not just AI shaking things up. We also have a whopping five generations working together right now, remote teams scattered across the world, and technology that connects us while leaving us more isolated. All of that is making workplaces much more complex.

Julia has observed these changes through her coaching work: "I think the friction created by change and so many generations working together is actually very good for people because through it, we grow and we evolve and we learn. We become better versions of ourselves. We just need leaders and teams who can grow, evolve, and learn alongside us; otherwise, we're just floundering."

When companies understand this, they really stop treating team building as entertainment. In a world where AI can handle routine tasks and automate processes, human connection *is* the competitive advantage.

Over the years, we've partnered with thousands of organizations, from startups to Fortune 500 companies like Apple, Microsoft, and Google. What unites them all isn't their size or industry. It's their recognition that team building has evolved from something you do because it seems like a good idea to something you do because your success depends on it. No matter who you are.

This Book Is for Every Team Player—Leaders, HR Pros, and Dreamers Alike

Whether you're running a Fortune 500 company or just trying to make your Mondays brighter, whether you're a leader, an HR pro, or a dreamer like me, you've come to the right place. This book will show you how to make work feel more human, help people connect and collaborate, and avoid the trap of checking boxes that so many businesses still fall into today.

Julia sums up what this journey is really about: "We all need to feel what we're doing matters. We need to know that there's something meaningful in our actions every single day, especially at work."

Great team building creates moments that matter, connections that stick, and reminds us why we show up.

The strategies, activities, and insights in this book aren't theory. They're battle-tested, field-proven approaches that have transformed thousands of teams. You'll learn the science behind why these methods work, the art of designing experiences that land, and the practical tools to make it happen, whether you have a big budget or are starting from scratch.

Welcome to *More Than Trust Falls.*

Let's play.

PART I

The Why Behind the Work

"You learn more about a person in an hour of play than in a year of conversation."

—Plato

When Plato wrote this observation of people, he didn't know how right he was. Thousands of years later, modern neuroscience, along with psychological research and brain imaging, confirms what he intuitively understood: play unlocks human connection.

This insight has driven everything we do at TeamBonding since day one. But it's not just about having fun (though that's essential too). It's about unlocking the potential of human connection and activating the brain in ways that spark creativity, ignite passion, build trust, and form deeper connections between colleagues. It's an incredibly fascinating thing to witness. It looks like magic, but it's really neuroscience in action.

The Question Everyone Asks

I get a lot of questions about my work when I tell people what I do. One of the more common ones is *why* team building actually works. Sure, from my enthusiasm and the size of the industry, it's obviously important, but people want to know what's really happening when teams play together. And it makes sense! After all, we're talking about creating conditions where lasting change, connection, and trust-building happen consistently, not accidentally.

That's exactly what I cover in this section. We're going to dig into the measurable neuroscience and psychology behind why play is essential for adults, what happens to people's brains when they learn to work together as a team, why connection matters more than you think, and how all of this translates into business results that'll turn your CFO's head.

To unpack the science behind all of this, I turned to someone who's spent his career turning connection into results.

Meet Your Guide: Tyler Hayden

As you saw in this book's introduction, I tapped my good friend Tyler Hayden for his insights here. He's a Hall of Fame keynote speaker, bestselling author, and TEDx presenter—and one of North America's most seasoned facilitators. He's delivered transformative experiences to everyone from local startups to Fortune 500 boardrooms to NASA rocket scientists.

When I sat down with Tyler to discuss this section, he cut through the noise with his deepest insight: "Good team building is good team learning."

After decades delivering practical solutions across nearly every industry—from Vegas stages to virtual classrooms—Tyler has observed that teams that truly click share one critical element: each member feels secure, supported, and engaged. And that comes directly from how their leaders show up.

To get leaders to show up, though, you have to speak their language.

Why This Matters to Your Bottom Line

Now that's a message that turns heads in business settings. My clients always lean in when I mention the bottom line, which is exactly why Tyler frames engagement in terms every business leader understands: "We all need more staff, right? More people committed to achieving our collective goals? Engagement essentially creates more staff from the staff you already paid for."

Increasing engagement by just 10% in a team of 10 means you now have the equivalent of one additional full-time employee's worth of productivity. In a world where employee engagement is at an all-time low, this represents a massive competitive advantage—unlocking dormant potential in the teams you've already invested in and assembled.

What You'll Discover in Part I

- ◆ **Chapter 1: The Power of Play**—Learn why play isn't just for children, but a powerful catalyst that sparks learning, innovation, connection, and engagement for adults, and it activates parts of the brain that many traditional methods simply can't.
- ◆ **Chapter 2: The Science of Connection**—Explore the real science behind connection and how it changes our brains when we bond, collaborate, and relax around one another, plus the neuroscience and evolutionary reasons why belonging builds better businesses.
- ◆ **Chapter 3: From Engagement to Impact**—Discover my secrets for turning this knowledge into engagement and tangible results to change how your team functions and how happy they are to show up every day.

Play. Connect. Engage. These three words are the key components behind why TeamBonding builds better teams.

CHAPTER 1

The Power of Play

Let's tackle the elephant in the room.

If there's one word that makes executives roll their eyes and employees groan, it's *play*.

This word makes people uncomfortable when used in a business context. When people are in working mode, they assume play is frivolous and unprofessional. I've heard every objection, usually something like:

> "We're adults, not kindergarteners. How is playing games going to help us hit our quarterly targets?"

Tyler Hayden says, "Fun is idiosyncratic. It's in the eye of the beholder."

His mantra is "team building is what you do with people, not to them." And I couldn't agree more. Resistance usually stems from forced fun that didn't align with how teams prefer to learn and engage.

In my experience, the people who resist play are the ones who need it most. And the companies that embrace it? They're the ones who pull ahead.

The Accidental Discovery

Like many epiphanies, I didn't discover this in a lab or through research. I discovered it by watching what happened during our events until the answer came to me.

I saw teams that had been struggling with communication suddenly working together effortlessly. I noticed colleagues who barely spoke started laughing, joking, and problem-solving with enthusiasm. I watched reserved employees stepping into leadership roles, their teams looking on in amazement.

The transformation wasn't happening despite the play—it was happening because of it.

I remember an accountant we'll call Allison, who never spoke in meetings, suddenly taking charge during a problem-solving challenge. It was so natural, I thought nothing of it when she started helping her team coordinate efforts, but I saw the look on her team lead's face and remembered him telling me how quiet she usually was. Watching that realization spread across his face was priceless, and Allison was promoted to project manager a few months later.

This moment started a shift in *how* I thought about what we were doing. I realized we weren't just entertaining people—we were tapping into something fundamental about how humans connect, learn, and grow.

We were proving the "adults don't play" myth wasn't just wrong, it was also costing businesses real money and opportunities.

Today, TeamBonding has worked with everyone from small startups to award-winning companies like Apple and Microsoft, and we've made the Inc. 5,000 list seven times by figuring out how to design events where play drives measurable business results.

Adults at Play: Breaking the Seriousness Myth

Corporate America clings to the myth that serious work requires serious people and serious behavior. This belief costs businesses millions every year in lost productivity, innovation, and talent. And most leaders are unaware.

Tyler sees it too: "People tend to be serious in meetings, but when they're in a safe space with peers, they let loose! It's natural. Leaders should lean into that." The key is understanding that resistance to play often comes from hierarchical dynamics, not aversion to engagement.

His approach? "Team learning progression. It's about de-inhibiting things like touch and laughter from social structure. This opens the door to growth just by getting people to relax and have fun together."

This reminded me of an event that involved more rubber chickens than I ever thought I'd see in one place.

We had a group of buttoned-up Fortune 500 executives, and we tasked them with racing rubber chickens through obstacle courses using props like pool noodles and hula hoops instead of their hands. Within minutes, these serious leaders were squeaking toys, army-crawling under tables in suits, and laughing like kids.

I watched as their social barriers fell to shared absurdity, and then the magic happened. By the end, they weren't just moving rubber chickens; they were solving complex challenges with trust, openness, and humility that usually takes years to build. They even kept a rubber chicken in their conference room as a reminder that sometimes the most productive thing you can do is stop taking yourself so seriously.

Think about the last time you had a genuine breakthrough at work. Not a time when you solved a routine problem, but a real "aha!" moment that changed everything. What were you doing and where were you when it happened? I'm guessing it wasn't during a formal presentation or (unless you were distracted and lost in thought) studying a spreadsheet. If you're like most people, it probably happened during a casual conversation, while walking, or joking with someone. There's a reason for that, and it goes back to how our brains work.

The Left Brain Trap

Most of us default to *serious work mode* in professional settings, and when we do, we're primarily using our left-brain hemisphere. This is the analytical, logical, step-by-step processing center. It's fantastic for executing known procedures and protocols, but terrible at making new, creative connections.

Most workplaces encourage and reward left-brain thinking because of those qualities. It's excellent for routines and hierarchies. But it's terrible for innovation and breakthroughs.

Creative solutions require the right brain for its imagination, pattern recognition, and leaps of intuition. And nothing activates the right brain like play.

When people engage with team building games and play, they remember how to tap into this part of their brain that's rarely used at work. People thought only artists, writers, and musicians benefited from right-brain thinking, but now it's recognized as vital to business success. After all, where would any successful enterprise be without innovative thinkers and creative problem-solving?

Ancient Wisdom, Modern Science

Using play as a learning tool isn't new. Chess, for instance, comes from a game called "chaturanga," developed in sixth-century India to train military leaders in strategy. It was preparation for life-and-death decisions on the battlefield.

We still see this today. Tyler once worked with a team of NASA rocket scientists who said they "never do team building." So, he chose an activity tailored to their sense of fun—quick, measurable, with a defined winner—and they had a blast. Why? Because he met them on their level with what they enjoyed.

Modern neuroscience has proven that our brains are incredibly receptive to play, and it's highly beneficial to social connections. Here's the neurochemistry that kicks in when people play together:

- **Dopamine Release:** Dopamine helps brains absorb and retain new information more effectively, especially during hands-on learning. Retention rates skyrocket.
- **Oxytocin Release:** Shared laughter triggers the "trust hormone," oxytocin. This makes the brain more receptive to collaboration, empathy, and risk-taking. Teams that laugh together develop stronger bonds at a neurological level.
- **Decrease of Stress Hormones[1]:** High levels of stress hormones like cortisol impair memory, reduce creativity, and cause people to view colleagues as threats. Most of us are very different people when stressed. Play decreases stress hormones, creating an optimal state for collaboration and innovation.

◆ **Neuroplasticity Stimulation:** The brain forms new neural pathways to keep up with novel experiences. This makes it easier to think in different ways and tap into creativity.

Play helps people feel more creative and connected, less stressed, and generally happier. This transforms group dynamics in ways traditional team building can't match.

When I was still new to team building, I watched a marketing team get *very* frustrated with a bridge-building challenge. Then their newest, quietest member started organizing materials and suggesting solutions, revealing herself as the strategic thinker they needed and didn't know they had. From there, they finished the challenge in minutes.

Why Play Works When Other Methods Don't

Most corporate training approaches tell people how to behave. "Communicate better." "Trust your teammates." "Be more innovative." But you can't think your way into new behaviors. You have to experience your way into them.

Tyler says, "Well-processed shared experiences are priceless. Every team activity is an opportunity to have a unique and shared experience that can be processed in a way that creates learning around a certain pre-established goal or objective."

He likes to use a structured, three-step approach to learning that embodies the power of play that he calls the "Adventure Wave."

1. **Briefing:** Talk to the group and set expectations
2. **Activity:** Start the event and create the shared play experience
3. **Extract:** Debrief and process the event

Play engages people. And, as Tyler likes to say, engagement literally gets more staff out of the staff you already have.

Play is the perfect way to make this happen, and your bottom line will thank you. Your teams will perform better, enjoy working together, and gain the context they need to learn new behaviors.

Engaging in play turns theory into practice, creating shared experiences that dissolve hierarchy and reinforce that experimentation is safe. When this happens, even failure becomes fun. These moments reveal people's authentic personalities, strengthen emotional bonds, and leave positive associations that carry into work.

That's why play works when other methods don't. It's not just an energizer—it's a transformative learning mechanism. Over the years, with the help of brilliant facilitators like Tyler, I've identified eight specific reasons why well-designed play drives measurable, lasting results. We're not talking feel-good benefits and mood boosters, but improvements that'll blow past your old productivity, retention, and innovation metrics with meaningful improvements to your bottom line.

Eight Reasons Play Drives Real Results

After decades of watching teams transform through play, I've seen the same patterns emerge over and over. It doesn't matter if I'm working with software engineers in Silicon Valley, nurses in Boston hospitals, or analysts on Wall Street; the benefits of play are remarkably consistent and powerful.

There's one thing separating play with the power to transform your crew from play that's forced on employees and gives team building a bad name: *intentionality.*

Making your team play a few random games in the meeting room might get some laughs, but it won't lead to lasting change. Along the same lines, rigid icebreakers might (big might) help people learn new things about colleagues, but it won't be genuine. At worst, they might feel so resistant that they don't learn anything.

The play experiences that create real business impacts are strategically designed to develop the capabilities teams need to succeed. Tyler uses the "3 F's," a framework he created, to ensure every event lands:

- ◆ **Fun:** Recreational, just-because activities for laughs and camaraderie
- ◆ **Fast-forward:** Learning and developing new skills, strategy, and business development
- ◆ **Fix:** Addressing dysfunctional teams, challenging relationships, and financial issues

Effective team building and playful activities rely on the latter two categories, and they're crafted to build powerful team dynamics.

Tyler creates metaphorms when designing activities, methods that compare adventure games to real-world applications. For example, *Minefield* is an activity intended for onboarding that uses mouse traps as "problems people experience," rubber chickens as "rewards people receive," with the new hire as a blindfolded walker who must rely on their leader's guidance to navigate terrain.

The magic isn't in the props, but the intentional parallels that make abstract business concepts tangible and memorable—which brings us back to the difference between random fun and strategic play. His metaphorms turn simple activities into powerful, intentional learning experiences teams can reference and apply long after the event ends.

Because these results are rooted in how people are wired, you're not forcing behavior change through willpower, threats, or compliance. You're creating conditions for better behaviors to emerge naturally, without your team even knowing it's happening.

Reason #1: Play Creates Deep, Active Learning

The best way to learn new skills is usually through hands-on action.

When your team is sitting in a room listening to a presentation, you'll be lucky if they remember 25% of what they hear. This is even more true if they're taking notes. It's easy to miss important points if you're always playing catch-up. Now there are AI recording and transcribing programs for this reason.

However, when participants engage in active learning by performing real-world tasks, collaborating with others, role-playing, or teaching colleagues, they retain significantly more because they're learning through memorable experiences.

It's Only Natural

When people are actively engaged, their brains form stronger neural pathways. The act of *doing* creates muscle, emotional, and cognitive memory simultaneously. It's how babies learn to walk, musicians learn to play, and leaders learn to guide teams. It's just how humans work.

Playing a team building game or working through a challenge gets people involved in the task in ways 99% of lectures never match. Sure, you might remember every second of an awe-inspiring speech your favorite professor gave, but outliers aren't the norm. No matter how long someone spends writing a presentation, our brains generally won't remember as well as a hands-on activity.

The research supports this. From the *American Journal of Play*: "Playing pays dividends by developing our mental, physical, and social skills. The insights we derive from 'This Little Piggy' and E=MC2 are both rooted in play. Rarely do we deliberately set out to learn by playing. Yet play educates us broadly and deeply early on and throughout our lives."[2]

In other words, whether we're learning to count toes or toying with thought experiments like Einstein, humans discover and understand the world through play—even if we don't think of it as learning.

The Lifelong Pattern of Learning Through Play

Think about how we learn during childhood. We master language through playful interactions. We explore numbers through games. We develop coordination by climbing trees or skipping rope. We discover nature by jumping in puddles or collecting shiny rocks.

When we play with others at any stage, we're finding our place in the world and developing our sense of self and our potential. Then these patterns get buried by adulting. We become wrapped up in being serious professionals. We stop enjoying things. We limit our potential. But when we regain our sense of play at work, we remember to tap into this learning mechanism.

I've watched hundreds of teams sit through hours of communication training and think they've improved, but their day-to-day interactions never change.

Put those same people in a challenge where they must guide a blindfolded teammate through an obstacle course using only their voice, and they immediately discover their communication gaps. They're forced to develop clearer language to succeed. And when they do, the dopamine rush cements those new skills more effectively than any PowerPoint could.

Reason #2: Play Removes the Fear of Failure

Tyler's approach to creating psychological safety through play is methodical. He sets ground rules like "challenge by choice," meaning voluntary participation, and "push past comfortable," which encourages stepping outside of comfort zones. This creates a safe environment where people can trust peers, explore, take risks, and make mistakes without real consequences.

This is part of why video games are a multi-billion-dollar industry and why we love sports. When you lose, it has zero impact on your career (unless you're playing professionally).

The brain also responds beautifully to mistakes. Mistakes have always taught us so much, dating back to people discovering what is and isn't safe to eat. Today, our mistakes may not have dire consequences, but some offices come close.

Employees should feel safe to make mistakes, and only leaders can make that happen. Research from the University of Georgia found that making, identifying, and correcting one's errors is associated with greater knowledge retention, improved learning, and better self-regulation.[3]

Historical examples support this. Edison failed more than 2,700 times creating the lightbulb, but he was also known for practical jokes and a playful nature.[4] His comfort with failure enabled breakthrough innovation. Similarly, one of Madame Curie's "failures" led to the discovery of radium. Columbus was looking for India when he found America.

If history isn't your thing, maybe this little Woody Allen quote will do: "If you're not failing every now and again, it's a sign you're not doing anything very innovative."

And Yet Leaders Still Punish Failure

Despite the evidence, many workplaces punish failure, which leads people to play it safe. If you have to weigh risk-taking against job security, it's smarter to stick to what you know. There might be better solutions, but why bother if you get fired or punished trying to find them?

Play helps create a consequence-free zone where teams can regain confidence by experimenting, failing, and learning. Giving your team a chance to fail in front of leadership during games helps them feel safer making mistakes in real scenarios. These experiences reinforce a culture of psychological safety.

In short, play teaches how to experiment and fail forward with confidence—exactly what organizations need to innovate and adapt.

Reason #3: Play Reveals Real-Time Team Dynamics

Play offers a way to reveal group dynamics in a controlled environment. It's a unique opportunity to see how people perform under pressure, work together, and where they need to improve. Every group develops a personality, but these dynamics are often invisible during everyday work.

How does the team communicate? Make decisions? Adapt to change? What roles do members naturally take?

You'll see these answers through play. Dynamics often masked by formal roles or stress become visible. Authentic patterns emerge as people step into leadership, find solutions, mediate conflicts, and keep the team focused.

Reason #4: Play Increases Self-Awareness by Revealing Hidden Strengths

Teams aren't the only things that can be evaluated during play—it's great for self-discovery too. Individuals learn about themselves and tap into hidden strengths. When team members try new things and take on new roles, they grow.

This self-examination is rare at work. Luckily, it's natural in play, and when you're having fun, your colleagues see your strengths too.

I can't count how many times I've heard, "I had no idea Emma was such a good leader!" or "Who knew Liam was so creative?" Sounds cheesy, sure, but people actually say this when they're having fun!

Real-World Benefits

This reminds me of a data analyst, Levi, who introduced himself as "just the numbers person" before an event. He went on to wow everyone by connecting patterns others missed. Levi's burst of creative problem-solving led him to volunteer for more creative projects—and he crushed them!

Levi shared strengths his team didn't know he had, and they helped him develop those strengths through more strategic and fulfilling roles. He felt more confident and secure, which reinforced belonging. When someone realizes they're integral—and their team knows it—they feel more solid.

These experiences also let colleagues reflect on moments when their teams couldn't have succeeded without them. These memories build confidence when facing new challenges.

Reason #5: Play Builds Trust Through Shared Vulnerability

What do you imagine when you think of teams building trust? If you're thinking of outdated trust falls and cheesy mantras, it's time to reassess, because that's not how trust is built.

Trust is created through shared experiences, especially ones involving vulnerability and relying on others. The benefits come from seeing colleagues struggle, laugh at mistakes, and support each other. That's when real bonds form and people begin to believe in one another.

Play naturally creates these opportunities. Sometimes the serious leader makes a silly mistake, and everyone starts laughing—not at them, but with them. These moments break down barriers and show everyone is human.

The Power of Looking Silly

Tyler says he's inspired to create environments where people "feel safe to look silly and take risks." That's the neurochemical process I'm talking about—shared vulnerability releases oxytocin, rewiring brains for collaboration.

Nothing bad ever came from realizing you can count on someone during a problem. These experiences develop genuine trust. The act of play—looking silly, laughing, and messing up—opens the door for it. It's about creating opportunities for trust to form organically, often without people realizing.

When you're having fun, you're not thinking, "My boss wants us to trust each other, how lame." There's no room for that when you're cheering on your colleague and want them to succeed—even if it's because you want your team to win. You're not thinking about your boss at all. You're watching teammates knock challenges out of the park and getting wrapped up in the games. It's a small but powerful difference.

Reason #6: Play Demonstrates the Value of Teamwork to Skeptics
Play is an excellent tool for showing skeptics the value of team-work. Chances are, you've worked with people who dislike working together and prefer to do everything alone. These people hesitate to share information, resources, or responsibilities, which isn't good.

I call them skeptics, and they inspire me to change their minds by creating opportunities to show them two heads are better than one. I love skeptics because I also love escape rooms.

Escape rooms are designed to be solved by a group within the time limit. That structure forces people to recognize and rely on teammates. They lead to results no one could've achieved alone—and they're great for skeptics.

Shining a Light on Diversity
Games that allow different ways to play together highlight the value of diversity. Like scavenger hunts for example. The more diverse the group, the more diverse the knowledge, which means a higher chance of success.

TeamBonding has designed many scavenger hunts where teams explore cities and complete challenges. We mix things up so colleagues find out who knows stuff they don't. That makes every person essential to success, especially when a leader shares team member details so we can customize the experience. If someone knows holidays, hobbies, or history from a culture others don't, they stand out. They're invaluable. It's beautiful, and if it sounds too good to be true, I promise you, it's not.

A few years ago, one facilitator told me about an ultra-competitive sales manager we'll call Jack, who insisted on working alone even though he'd been stuck on a puzzle for 30 minutes. He'd even called his teammates "weaker employees" before the event—yikes.

Then two colleagues helped Jack with what he'd been stuck on, and they solved it in two minutes using what he'd gathered. He left the event flabbergasted. At lunch afterward, Jack said, "I never realized how much faster we could move together. That was so weird!"

Jack's experience sticks with me because these are the moments I live for in this industry.

Reason #7: Play Creates Pleasure and Drives Performance

There's a direct correlation between pleasure and productivity. Why? Because play releases dopamine.

Enjoyment, or pleasure, is a powerful motivator for humans and animals alike. People perform better when they enjoy what they're doing, and why wouldn't they? They're happy, engaged, and motivated, which means that those pleasure chemicals are enhancing what the brain can do.

The pleasure from learning through play, being challenged, and thinking outside the box can revitalize a group, rebuild morale, create friendships, inspire self-confidence, and more. When people have fun together, stress decreases, creativity increases, and social bonds strengthen. Because they're enjoying themselves, they're committed and retain more knowledge.

I'm not talking about superficially making work more "fun" or just gamifying the workplace. This is about creating positive associations through collaboration, learning, and problem-solving. In my experience, teams that enjoy working together tend to be more resilient, creative, and committed when facing challenges and shared goals.

Reason #8: Play Deliver Specifics, Customizable Learning Outcomes

One of the most important things to me with TeamBonding is customizing experiences to meet team needs. We don't use cookie-cutter events. We work with people to discover *who* their team members are, *what* they hope to gain, *when* the issues started, *where* they'd like to play, and *why* they want team building. We also learn about their company and industry.

Then, we design a play experience to deliver specific lessons, skills, and outcomes tailored to their needs. Some focus on group dynamics and collaboration. Others target individual skills like communication or leadership. Many involve problem-solving or emphasize physical coordination and trust. And if we don't have an activity that fits, we make one.

The Flexibility Advantage

The beauty of play-based learning is its flexibility. Need to improve communication? There are activities that highlight communication challenges and allow practice. Want to develop leadership skills? Use games that create safe leadership experiments with real-time feedback.

This is what separates professional team building from random games. Every element is designed with purpose and intentionality, targeting specific learning goals using proven structures. The play isn't the goal—it's the vehicle for achieving tangible business outcomes.

Overcoming the Fear of Judgment Through Play

Despite these advantages, many people still resist play as a method of team building. Fear of judgment is one primary barrier I often see that prevents people from engaging, even when they know the benefits. But even though fear of judgment is a frequent concern holding people back from embracing play, it's also one that fun is best at helping people overcome.

Before we move on, here are some stats worth considering: 56% of all employees say anxiety often impacts their workplace performance,[5] and 97% of people between 25 and 34 fear colleagues will judge their communication.[6]

Why does this matter? Because these are more than comfort issues—they're productivity killers.

How Fear Holds Teams Back

Much like pleasure, fear is a powerful motivator for humans and most living things. The fear of being judged is overwhelming for many adults, and it's a common sight in the workplace. When it affects a person, you'll see several patterns emerge:

Overthinking and Second-Guessing

Unless you're one of the lucky ones, you're probably aware of how many hours you can spend drafting and redrafting simple emails, and how many days you can spend rehearsing presentations, ideas for meetings, or responses to questions, even if it's just in your car while stuck in traffic. This pattern creates mental paralysis, preventing you from being present and showcasing your potential.

Avoidant Behavior

Another natural habit we exhibit in response to fear is avoidance. This tendency helped humans stay alive and evolve. However, we're not trying to survive in the wild anymore when we go to work, and this instinct doesn't serve us. When people are afraid at work, they shy away from opportunities and challenges that would benefit them. They might decline leadership roles, opt out of complex projects, or retreat when creative input is required.

Physical Stress Responses

Extreme or persistent fear can cause headaches, a racing heart, trouble sleeping, muscle tension, and difficulty focusing.

If these patterns sound like anxiety, that's because it is. Consistent work-related stress and fear can lead to anxiety, and existing anxiety can worsen these issues. And sadly, it has the potential to impair performance and decision-making.

All of this leads to missed opportunities and stifled creativity. People can't innovate when they're too afraid to share ideas. Teams can't solve problems when members won't risk being wrong. Companies can't evolve when everyone's playing it safe.

The Workplace Fear Cycle

I want you to imagine that you're on a team working on a HUGE project that's essential to your company. Your boss hand-picked each team member to handle the project, including you. Obviously, you've demonstrated capabilities that proved to your boss you can get this done.

But you're not thinking about that.

You're thinking about how important this task is, and you're worried you're not good enough to do it. Imagine spiraling into how disappointed your boss will feel if you fail. How upset you'll make your team. What if you lose your job? Maybe not getting fired for failing, but if the company needs to make cuts? You assume your boss will put you on the chopping block because you couldn't meet his expectations.

And the spiral doesn't stop there. Your thoughts circle the drain to less-likely situations until you're paralyzed by it. Despite ever-present fear in your mind, though, you buckle up and do the next task on your to-do list anyway. But since you were distracted by fear, your work is full of mistakes you overlooked, and they come up during a meeting. Now you're starting to think those fears might not just be in your head after all. . .

This is the fear cycle, and it'll likely repeat throughout the project. Your worries get worse each time mistakes are addressed, which impacts your work more every time. It'll likely resurface from project to project until it becomes a self-fulfilling prophecy. Until, of course, you lose your job. Or, worse, quit because you can't take it anymore.

The fear cycle is often tied up in a tangled knot of fear of being judged, fear of failure, and fear of consequences. Depending on its severity, that knot might even include fear of ruining your whole life, disappointing your family, and so on.

The fear of being judged for making mistakes is real, and most of us experience it to some degree at some point in our careers. But we all make mistakes, and we can't let fear of a potential mistake stop us from trying.

Office Anxiety

Another manifestation of the fear cycle is the anxiety many feel surrounding creativity and innovation. You need to share ideas—good, mediocre, or ineffective—if you want to create something innovative with your team.

- **Ineffective ideas** help identify what to avoid and what won't work. They're part of the process in many industries, and magic won't happen without them.
- **Mediocre ideas** can often be refined into good ones. They might inspire an epiphany or shine a light on a bad idea.
- **Good ideas** are obvious gold. They help teams move forward by leaps and bounds.

Many feel anxious their ideas will be ridiculed or rejected, and this causes them to lose sight of the importance of contributing. As a result, teams miss out on opportunities to grow. While this is most common in toxic work environments where communication isn't encouraged, it can happen to anyone.

The Risks of Fear at Work

I'm not saying fear and anxiety are always bad feelings in daily life or work. They're natural. You shouldn't be down on yourself or colleagues for feeling these emotions. That said, fear of failure is more than a momentary concern, especially in the office. This psychological barrier can hold you back, prevent you from achieving potential, and do the same to your team. That's why leaders should be vigilant when it starts impacting even one person.

It's easy to get trapped in a fear cycle or a pattern of hesitation, and that can spread like an infection, leading people to avoid risks and miss opportunities to achieve goals.

How Play Creates Psychological Safety

The power of play is, in large part, the ability to create psychological safety, an important aspect to ensuring team members feel comfortable being vulnerable, asking questions, making mistakes, and failing. People need to do all of these things for a team to reach its full potential. Even one can cause a ripple effect that impacts your culture and bottom line:

- **Lack of vulnerability** leads to an inability to connect.
- **Fear of asking questions** leads people to operate on incomplete information.
- **Fear of making mistakes** leads to teams avoiding trying new things.
- **Fear of failure** leads to anxiety that creates sub-optimal outcomes.
- **Failure and ridicule resulting from the above** leads to reaffirming fearful beliefs, amplifying the fear cycle.

This is why you never want someone afraid of messing up. Your team should exist free from negative consequences for the mistakes that happen when people try new things.

The most successful companies understand this. Their upper management knows people must fail before they succeed because they've been there. These people create cultures that embrace failure, often using play as a natural lab for learning.

One of my favorite clients runs a tech startup that made "failure parties" part of their culture. At these celebrations, teams are rewarded for their biggest mistakes with cake, champagne, and a relaxed afternoon sharing what they learned. This client doubled their rate of innovation and growth because people started solving problems faster and felt more comfortable admitting mistakes.

Making Play Work for Your Organization

As I've pointed out every time I poke fun at trust falls, not all play is created equal. "Mandatory fun" can damage team dynamics because it's not enjoyable, and no one wants to participate.

I've outlined five practical points that can make your team's experiences enjoyable while driving real results.

Start with Purpose

Every activity should connect to specific business goals. Are you trying to improve communication? Build trust? Enhance creativity? Practice adaptability? Choose activities that develop these skills.

Example: Instead of generic team building, a hospital chose communication-focused activities after some patient handoff errors that directly addressed their issue. The results were so good, they made it a quarterly event.

Make It Voluntary

Forced participation defeats the purpose. It's important to create opportunities for play and allow people to engage at their comfort levels.

Example: A law firm offered three options during their retreat and allowed everyone to choose what worked for them. Introverts picked strategy games, extroverts picked high-energy challenges, and outdoorsy types chose physical games. This became their annual format after receiving positive feedback.

Focus on Experience, Not Content

The exact activity matters less than the experience it creates. Look for activities that foster genuine interaction, give people opportunities to overcome challenges together, and celebrate both success and failure.

Example: We custom-made a simple blindfolded assembly task, followed by trivia and a happy hour for a manufacturing team.

This revealed more about their communication gaps than any workshop ever had, and the client reported great success afterward.

Debrief Thoughtfully

Teams learn when they reflect and share their thoughts. What did they notice about their communication? How did they handle unexpected challenges? What strengths emerged that they can leverage at work?

Example: After a pub crawl scavenger hunt (one of my all-time favorite events) in DC, an engineering team realized they'd fallen into work silos and discussed it at dinner, where we ended the event. The feedback we received indicated that cross-team collaboration had improved significantly afterward.

When lockdown hit, we recreated this experience with a virtual mixology class, which had equally profound results.

Follow Through Consistently

One-off activities create temporary good feelings, but regular play builds transformation. Let team members continue learning and bonding through regular events.

Example: A marketing agency did a fun event building a miniature golf course from canned goods and non-perishable packaged food items later donated to a food bank. They enjoyed it so much that they began 15-minute creative challenges every Friday and TeamBonding events every other month. They maintained the mindset and became regulars we still have today.

My Bottom Line on Play

I've spent decades learning about play and connection, and realized it's essential for collaboration, cooperation, communication, and creativity. Employees need to take risks without fear of reprisal, trust each other to try new things, and let loose together. Destressing is as crucial as upskilling, and a well-designed event can do both.

The business leaders who understand this—the ones who emphasize connection, play, and exploration—are the ones operating thriving companies. They attract top talent, outshine the competition, and enjoy the process. They know play isn't the opposite of serious work; it's part of it.

It's the colleagues who play together that trust and take risks together. They communicate better, solve problems faster, and become more resilient. In doing so, they grow into something greater than the sum of their parts: honest, open, and connected teams that exude energy when they walk into a room.

Tyler really gets this, and it's one reason I asked him to help write the first section. He captured something essential when he framed "team building" as "team learning," and it changed how I approach every event we run.

Our clients at TeamBonding aren't paying for recreation—they're investing in skill development that's also enjoyable.

Succeeding in the corporate world is about how quickly and effectively teams can adapt, innovate, and execute. If you want your company to stay on top, it starts with your people. They drive everything and treating them accordingly is how you keep them engaged and attract top talent.

The science is clear, the results are measurable, and the path forward is simple: if you want high-performing teams and a successful company, start with play and build from there.

CHAPTER 2

The Science of Connection

I hope our journey through the power of play has given you a new perspective on why adults need opportunities to have fun, let loose, and laugh together. We need to engage, experiment, and fail as a team, and you'll see tons of benefits if you make time for this with your people.

Play activates our right brain, fosters psychological safety, and builds trust through shared vulnerability. If you're like me, you probably want to know why this works. What's really going on in our brains when we feel connected, especially at work?

The answer lies in the science of human connection. Neurochemistry, psychology, and our evolutionary wiring for cooperation and belonging. To understand all of this, we'll go on a journey through the worlds of team psychology, group dynamics, and human instincts that drive us to seek connection.

We'll explore how teams form, why belonging matters, and what trust looks like on a neurochemical level. You'll see why play is the most efficient way to activate the human brain's capacity for collaboration, learning, and growth.

The science behind connection explains why the techniques we explored in Chapter 1 are so remarkably effective, and I hope this inspires you to implement them yourself.

What I've Learned About Connection

With my years of watching teams transform (or completely fall apart), I've come to realize that most leaders are "certain" they understand what makes teams work. They focus on factors like goals, communication, and strategy while missing the basic necessity for connection.

When colleagues *click*, an invisible web forms. You see it in their body language, how they finish each other's sentences, and the energy they bring into a room. Others notice it in their work, notes, unique insights, and the questions they ask.

I'm sure you'd scoff at it in a movie, thinking to yourself, "Yeah, right, I *wish*." But trust me, it's *real*.

Without the right environment, that web never forms, and employees will struggle even when they're working side by side. Or worse, the web tangles into misunderstandings, mistrust, and missed opportunities.

Like a dark reflection of the well-connected team, a tangled web will be evident in your team's body language, interactions, and energy when they enter a room. It won't be pretty, and others will notice it, too.

The science of connection isn't as simple as getting along. It goes deeper than that, into the inner workings of how the human brain is wired for connection and collaboration. Connection is literally at the core of who we are as a species, not in our office politics or workplace roles. We built these skills way back when teamwork was essential to take down a big animal to feed our families without anyone getting injured or killed.

Once you understand how this works, you can create the conditions needed to build an unbreakable web of connections with your team and cultivate an environment where true collaboration happens with intention.

We're going to explore this science through three critical lenses:

- ◆ **The Psychology of Teams:** First, we'll dive into the psychology of how people form connections. This is all about group dynamics, relationships, and leadership patterns that either build bridges or walls between people.
- ◆ **Why Belonging Builds Better Businesses:** Next, we'll examine why belonging has become the secret weapon within high-performing organizations, and how diversity, equity, inclusion, and belonging are keystones of connection and genuine success.

◆ **Neuroscience and the Play Advantage:** Finally, we'll take a look at the neuroscience behind it all. Here, you'll learn about what's happening in the human brain when someone is connected and feels like they're a part of something bigger.

Once you understand the science of connection from these angles, you'll probably want to stop leaving team chemistry to chance. It's my goal to give you a better idea of how to create connection and chemistry with intentionality after reading this chapter.

The Psychology of Teams

Sometimes, when fate aligns, teams click instantly. Others struggle for months to find their groove or never connect at all. The difference? Group dynamics, interpersonal relationships, leadership, and (you guessed it) team building.

Tyler sees this in action across industries, and he wastes no words: "It comes down to leadership. Are they authentic? Do team members feel secure, supported, and engaged? Do they show up for their colleagues? Are people involved in the strategy? Does everyone have the tools they need to succeed?"

Tyler emphasizes the *psychology of flow*, the balance between challenge and skill. "When teams are engaged in purposeful work that provides a good level of challenge with enough room to relax, they thrive," he explains. This is the sweet spot where people lose themselves in meaningful and engaging work that keeps them fully absorbed, energized, and performing at their peak. All without burning out from constant pressure or disengaging because the tasks are too easy.

Teams that achieve this flow state don't just get more done—they also change how they relate to each other. To understand this correlation, we need only look at the invisible forces shaping every team interaction: group dynamics.

Group Dynamics

While there are multiple academic and sociological ways to define "group," all it really means is two or more people with some form of social connection. A family of four is a group, and so is a stadium of football fans, but these two collections of people function and relate to each other in very different ways.

Groups can be broken down into four categories:

- **Intimacy groups:** Families, close friends, romantic partners
- **Weak associations:** Concert audiences, passengers on a train, people waiting for a bus
- **Social categories:** Broad groups like "Americans" or "Christians"
- **Task groups:** Work teams, sports teams, project groups

We focus on task groups—teams formed with a purpose. These groups need clear communication, authentic trust, and interdependence. They also require more structure than, say, a group of strangers waiting for the same bus.

Depending on the group's leadership style, you might see one person calling all the shots, tasks flowing from person to person like a relay race, or roughly equal responsibility between members. Perhaps information moves from managers to leaders, to mediators, and finally to the team, or maybe it's shared directly among all members in group meetings.

Tyler calls this the *Princess Bride principle*. He explains that fighting one person is different than fighting a group. A 20-person startup has more entrepreneurial energy, while a Fortune 500 has more bureaucratic energy. Both are valid, but they require different approaches to meet their teams' psychological needs.

Think of this "energy" as the flow of information, decisions, and collaboration through your organization. It's essential to examine what blocks that flow, what activates it, and what carries it forward. Structure can either help or hinder, depending on the outcomes the team is after.

I've seen teams with identical goals and resources perform separately and produce dramatically different results. It comes down to how people interact within their group structure. Some folks naturally support others, stepping in to mediate conflicts, what have you—they're gold. Others block communication, shift blame, or are *too* accommodating just to move things forward. They're not bad, but they do have bad habits.

Everyone brings different experiences to the table, with strengths and weaknesses that dictate how well they perform in specific roles. The good news is that people can improve weak skills and let their existing strengths shine with the right exercises and activities.

One trick I've learned about improving task groups is to identify those with personality traits that encourage smooth workflow and put them in positions where those strengths are most useful. When your structure places everyone in a position where their strengths shine, relationship dynamics, interdependence, and trust improve, fostering stronger interpersonal relationships.

Interpersonal Relationships

The human need for connection dates back to our earliest ancestors. Strong emotional bonds helped them survive, which is why companionship became one of our most basic needs.

While connection is evolutionary, though, social skills are learned. That means the way we interact varies from person to person. This learning begins with our first encounters with groups and social relationships, typically with our families. The culture we're raised in also shapes us throughout our lives.

As we grow up, we're exposed to more people and make new connections. We go from immediate and extended families to our parents' friends and coworkers, and other children in those circles, then to neighborhoods and schools. From these early social bonds, we begin to form a sense of right and wrong and learn how our actions affect others. Because we all grow up differently, though, we connect, communicate, and relate in our own ways.

The trick is to help people connect, even though everyone grew up with vastly different experiences and communication styles. That means cultivating empathy, understanding, and interpersonal bonds to strengthen relationships between team members.

The stronger the interpersonal relationships, the better the communication between team members.

One behavioral study states: "The positive effects of high-quality workplace relationships on working manners include higher commitment, lower level of reported job stress, and increased perception of social impact."[1]

I think of all relationships as having an emotional "carrying capacity," which is my way of saying there's a limited amount of positive and negative emotions any relationship can withstand without feeling strained. Stronger relationships have greater emotional carrying capacities, which means better support systems and stronger groups.

Tyler frames this in terms of what he calls the *piggy bank principle*. "It starts with making daily investments in your team members and social relationships," he explains. "With each investment, you're putting another coin in the piggy bank. Then, during times of change, which often lead to periods of stress and fear, you take out some of those coins of trust that you've been putting in and use them to reassure, demonstrate authenticity, and remind your crew that you care."

Psychological Safety: The Foundation for Connection

In Chapter 1, I said people need to feel psychologically safe before team belonging and emotional intelligence can be effective.

Everyone on the team should feel certain that they'll *never* face embarrassment, rejection, or punishment for sharing ideas, asking for feedback, taking risks, or making mistakes. You can't expect people to have the confidence and courage to speak up or try something innovative in an environment where they face consequences for missteps and differing opinions.

If you disagree, I challenge you to start thinking about human psychology through a lens of compassion instead of business or power.

The numbers around psychological safety are staggering. Workers who feel psychologically safe are 50% more productive, 76% more engaged, 57% more likely to collaborate, and 76% less stressed than those in psychologically unsafe environments.[2] Additionally, those workplaces have 27% less turnover.

When your team members feel safe enough to be themselves without fear, to share their ideas and take risks on potentially innovative ideas without any worries of being humiliated or punished, you'll start to see the magic of connection taking hold in a tangible way. And the impact on your bottom line will put you ahead of the competition.

I've seen this play out with many teams, and it's almost immediately apparent when people start to connect.

When a team is psychologically safe, strong communication and conversations flow freely. People are comfortable with giving and, more importantly, *receiving* constructive feedback without defensiveness. This boosts morale, especially when leaders model the same vulnerability and courage.

When psychological safety is missing, most team building activities fall flat. Everyone's too busy protecting themselves to genuinely connect, and everyone is defensive. All you get is forced conversation, fear of judgment, and a low-energy vibe. Why? Because the moment these people return to the office, they're back to feeling like someone's waiting for them to slip up. They know the safety created by that event, no matter how fun and well-designed, is temporary.

Teams need psychological safety because the alternative is unsustainable. This process begins with leaders modeling the behavior they want to see: communicating openly, listening to criticism, including everyone, and showing vulnerability.

If your company culture fosters safety, team building becomes invaluable because it creates low-risk environments where people can practice these things and learn to trust this newfound safety when they return to the office. They become comfortable with vulnerability, risk-taking, and being supportive. Instead of feeling like a farce, team building acts as training wheels for psychological safety, creating a strong foundation for this behavior at work.

Leadership

Leadership is about creating safe environments and facilitating effective communication among all members, not authority.

Tyler's worked with leaders using all kinds of approaches throughout his career, and he's seen the weight they carry on their shoulders. They're the ones who can make or break a team. It's up to them to form that web of connection and help everyone feel secure, supported, and engaged.

While the debates about which leadership style works best are endless, I've noticed some patterns about what makes it easier to carry this weight, show up for your team, and build a healthy culture where everyone thrives:

- **Average Leadership Style (ALS)** is the most familiar, with a single person in charge of everyone else. Ideally, they treat everyone equally and fairly. This approach can work great for smaller groups, but it becomes challenging with larger ones because the focus shifts to the leader's needs, rather than the team's. Many modern leadership styles have moved away from ALS, favoring styles that emphasize group needs and relationships.

- **Leader Member Exchange (LMX)** flips this on its head. LMX focuses on the relationships between the leader and each team member. Instead of the one-size-fits-all approach, the leader builds complex and genuine connections with everyone individually. But, like ALS, this approach is challenging in larger groups. At that point, it's better to create smaller groups with their own leaders.

- **Complex Leadership Theory (CLT)** distances itself from traditional leadership, recognizing that leaders exist organically, not just within hierarchies. While there might be a formal "leader," everyone is encouraged to take charge when the situation calls for it. For example, during periods of change, members of CLT groups may naturally start helping others to keep everyone on target. This ability to adjust leadership is what distinguishes CLT structures from traditional hierarchies.

LMX and CLT both excel at handling adaptive challenges better than traditional and rigid leadership styles. In the words of professor and author Ronald A. Heifetz, "Adaptive challenges are problems that require new learning, innovation, and new patterns of behavior. They are different from technical problems, which can be solved with knowledge and procedures already in hand."[3]

Regardless of leadership style, the ability to foster communication remains critical:

- ◆ **In ALS,** it's imperative that all group members receive clear direction and equal paths of communication.
- ◆ **In LMX,** the relationship between leaders and members depends on clear exchanges between the parties.
- ◆ **In CLT,** leadership develops and thrives most in situations where communication channels are clear and group members can help one another.

Whether it's equal paths for everyone, individual exchanges, or leadership that emerges naturally, clear communication makes the web of connection work. That's the secret to a group that just *clicks*.

This sparks follow-up questions: what makes those lines of communication strong? Is it just the relationships and their emotional capacity that matter?

Team Building for Leadership Development

Now everything starts coming together!

How do team building experiences improve group dynamics, relationships, and leadership? It's all about the psychology of teamwork and what transforms a loose collection of coworkers into a strong, effective team.

Most teams undergo a predictable life cycle standardized into five distinct stages:

1. Forming

Here, team members are figuring out where they fit in. They're learning what relationships they'll have with one another, what roles they'll fulfill, and how they feel about what this group will do in the future.

This is prime time for icebreakers and activities that help them get to know each other and form a well-functioning team. Activities should reflect these goals so they can start developing genuine bonds.

2. Storming

At this point, storms begin forming. People get comfortable enough to push back and test boundaries. Personalities clash and conflict strikes—which is perfectly normal and part of being human!

Every group, of all ages, experiences this. The key is keeping open lines of communication and providing the tools everyone needs to get through the friction. It's all about finding compromises, solutions, and common ground so they can move to the next phase.

3. Norming

Here's where teams hit their stride and leave friction behind. Authentic social connections and friendships should begin growing.

Now's the time for activities like scavenger hunts, problem-solving, and exploratory fun. You want to improve developing bonds and strengthen communication in a more relaxed environment.

> **Pro Tip:** If new conflicts arise during norming, don't panic! Many teams cycle between norming to storming a few times before moving on. It's normal. Try to help them connect with some extra team building events and casual socialization activities like happy hour.

4. Performing

This is the sweet spot we're looking for! Team members are working well together, people understand their roles, and they move toward goals enthusiastically. You'll see strong interpersonal relationships, especially if everyone is comfortable with their position and leadership.

As long as your team stays here, focus efforts on reinforcing bonds through activities. Community service projects are great because, as we'll discuss in Chapter 8, charity work is incredibly effective at helping people build deep, meaningful connections while building skills.

5. Transforming

This stage pops up when the team completes large goals, shifts directions, or changes members. The team might be dissolving, reorganizing, or starting new projects.

If it's a big enough change, they'll go all the way back to Forming, and the cycle will repeat. Smaller changes may send the team back to Storming or Norming.

Understanding these stages brings us to perhaps the most critical element of modern team dynamics: belonging.

Belonging Builds Better Businesses

Now we understand how team psychology works. So let's talk about what obstacles get in the way of connection, and the primary element to overcome them: *belonging*.

I've watched teams of talented individuals completely underperform, and it's usually because some or all of the members don't feel like they belong in the group.

Meanwhile, teams comprised of beginners and experts can crush their goals and make it look easy because everyone feels valued, heard, and capable. They trust that they belong.

This contrast highlights the true power of belonging.

According to McKinsey, companies that get this right, those that are diverse and inclusive, are 35% more likely to outperform their competitors.[4] But a toxic workplace where people feel excluded and believe they don't belong will kill employee well-being, teamwork, creativity, and profits.

Fostering the Existential

Developing something as intangible as belonging can feel overwhelming, especially to those who rely on metrics. You can't put a number on a deeply personal experience like belonging.

Belonging is often tied to a person's core beliefs about how the world responds to their actions. It's a vulnerable topic tied to the sense of self, and it sits at the intersection of community, acceptance, and identity. Many people need years of personal reflection, growth, and even talk therapy to truly feel a consistent sense of belonging.

But don't get discouraged. Even if you don't feel belonging in daily life, you can experience it with a group of people you trust and respect. That's part of *why* social circles lift us up!

"Believing that they're part of something comes when people are known and seen," explains Tyler. "They're appreciated for their strengths and supported in challenging times. Remember, team members are as diverse as the devices they carry—each one might have a phone, but most have different models. Likewise, each person's viewpoint is truly unique."

Belonging doesn't (always) stem from shared similarities. People find true belonging in groups where everyone wants each other to be authentic and will support them no matter what.

It's All About Diversity, Equity, Inclusion, and Belonging (DEIB)

The idea of diversity, equity, inclusion, and belonging has been floating around corporate America for years now. They're wonderful words and concepts, which makes it easy to glaze over what DEIB is all about or to dismiss it as unrealistic, which doesn't help *anyone*.

Let's break down how each word applies to real teams. We're not just looking at definitions (I'm not rewriting the dictionary), but how these words help teams connect.

Diversity

Diversity is about differences in gender, race, culture, upbringing, background, thinking styles, learning styles, personal experiences— the works. It's about all the differences and similarities people bring to the community you serve, your marketplace, and your workforce.[5]

People's inherent differences strengthen teams by enriching the variety of experiences and perspectives. It's like the story about the blind men and the elephant I told in the introduction, and the entire reason I've interviewed experts like Tyler throughout this book— when you have people looking at things from different angles, you improve creativity and ensure you're seeing the bigger picture.

Take the old adage "two heads are better than one" and crank it up to eleven.

Equity

Equity concerns fairness, but it's not the same as equality. We acknowledge the world isn't fair and that not everyone starts or experiences life with the same opportunities and resources as others. Equity is about leveling the playing field (see Figure 2.1).

EQUALITY **VS** **EQUITY**

Figure 2.1 This image has stayed with me since the first time I saw it, and it's my go-to for explaining equity in a snap.

One example of the lack of equity is degree requirements for jobs. Many people don't get to attend college, but that doesn't mean they can't excel and outperform their college-educated peers. Companies that strive for equity often eliminate once-stringent degree requirements, shifting the focus to a candidate's ability to fulfill the role. At the very minimum, this looks like "Bachelor's degree **or equivalent experience**."

Inclusion

Inclusion is how you nurture the feeling of psychological safety and connection with peers. Inclusive environments help everyone feel accepted, valued, supported, and listened to. People believe they have a voice to communicate freely and be heard.

When companies successfully create inclusive environments, you see workplaces with happy, confident, and innovative teams. These teams demonstrate better productivity and, in many cases, a strong sense of company loyalty.

Belonging

You can't create genuine diversity, equity, and inclusion without belonging.

When you do, though, your people know they're valued and can connect to their team members *and* their workplace. People will feel driven, confident, and motivated, leading to a happier, more productive, and more profitable workplace.

DEIB Isn't a Nice-To-Have, It's a Must-Have

The numbers don't lie. According to Glassdoor, 69% of executives say diversity and inclusion are important,[6] and 63% of employees prioritize DEIB programs when job hunting—that jumps to 73% for Gen Z workers.[7]

Sounds like a no-brainer, right? Yeah, it does to me, too.

But DEIB efforts still face serious challenges in today's workplaces. I see resistance to change, a lack of awareness, inadequate policies, and even a fixation on political differences blocking progress toward creating equitable and inclusive workplaces.

I've also seen TeamBonding's events help teams realize why DEIB matters. Sometimes I get to watch little lightbulbs glow as people experience DEIB in action for the first time. No matter how many times they've listened to boring lectures about the topic, it's the first-hand experience that makes it click.

The Business Case for Belonging

Since I've encountered so many people who scoff at this, I'll give you five concrete ways building belonging drives results:

1. **Belonging Enhances Innovation and Creativity:** Diverse teams solve problems better and faster. Homogeneous groups tend to recycle ideas and get stuck. Meanwhile, diverse teams unlock breakthroughs and run circles around competitors, all thanks to their fresh perspectives.

2. **It Boosts Retention and Engagement:** Employees who feel they belong go the extra mile to support the place where they're respected and happy. You wouldn't want a company to fail when it's created the best environment you've ever worked in, would you? That's why retention and engagement soar when companies focus on DEIB.

3. **It Supercharges Productivity:** When people feel supported and happy, they perform better. Groups that get along and trust each other get more done because they're busy clicking, not clashing. Psychological safety and connection make people care more, try new things, and push harder to overcome challenges.

4. **It Builds a Better Brand:** Inclusive workplaces attract top talent, loyal customers, and glowing reputations. A company culture of belonging is a magnet for excellence, goodwill, and trust. These places have shining Glassdoor reviews that make top talent clamor for open positions. This reputation also makes customers want to support the brand.

5. **It Reveals Blind Spots:** Diverse teams prevent costly oversights by empowering people to speak up. There's a famous legend about a car company that named a model the "Nova." It performed well in the US but flopped in Latin America. Why? In Spanish, "no va" means "no go"—they literally marketed a "no-go" car! A culturally diverse and aware team would've immediately caught that blunder.

Building Your Belonging Strategy

With all the benefits of DEIB and making sure people feel like they belong, I hope you're excited to see it in action! Creating a workplace that emphasizes these qualities doesn't happen overnight, but it might be easier than you expect.

If you're workplace lacks these things, these measures can get the ball rolling:

1. **Get leadership buy-in first:** Leadership needs to be committed to diversity and inclusion. Change happens from the top down.

2. **Assess where you are now:** Know the current state to focus efforts and track progress.

3. **Assemble a diverse team to lead the effort:** Walk the talk, include diverse representatives in the planning process.

4. **Set clear, measurable objectives:** Know exactly how and when to celebrate your wins to keep momentum.

5. **Create a written plan:** A step-by-step plan keeps everyone aligned and accountable.

6. **Work toward your goals together:** Start doing team building exercises and getting everyone involved in activities to help you achieve your DEIB goals.

Connected teams are more likely to embrace DEIB initiatives because they've already built a foundation of trust, and they're typically eager to put these plans into action.

This is why I've developed programs specifically to strengthen bonds between colleagues. As they grow and connect, they'll organically place more value on diversity, equity, inclusion, and belonging. Then, when you pitch a DEIB program, they're primed to jump in!

It's an ongoing process that fortifies the web of connection and moves you closer to having a team that works together like they're in a movie. They'll be finishing each other's sentences, walking into meetings with confidence, and wowing everyone with their work in no time. And your competition will envy them (and you).

The Neuroscience Behind It All

Everything we've talked about, from group psychology to belonging to emotional intelligence, is all happening in your brain in real, measurable ways. When I tell skeptical executives that team building isn't just fluff, this is what I mean. There's neuroscience behind why some teams click and others don't.

I've spent decades watching emotional intelligence (EI) evolve from a novel concept to a core business necessity. In the 1990s, when I'd mention EI to leaders, I'd get quizzical looks. These days, it's more universal because leaders have realized how essential it's become.

What Emotional Intelligence Really Means

When I talk about EI, I'm referring to awareness of your emotions and feeling able to express them freely. This includes managing your interpersonal relationships at work with fairness and empathy. Here are just a few examples:

- Handling frustration without losing your cool
- Reading the room when you walk into a meeting
- Expressing concerns at work without creating conflict
- Setting healthy boundaries while respecting those of others

A Niagara Institute study found that emotional intelligence was the strongest predictor of performance out of 34 workplace skills.[8] It also showed that employees with emotionally intelligent managers are four times less likely to quit their jobs.

Why? Our emotional responses are interwoven into everything we do. They've influenced almost every decision you've made, every interaction you've had, and every thought that's crossed your mind.[9] Like it or not, this is how our brains are wired.

There are huge perks to creating a company culture that emphasizes emotional intelligence, too. It improves creativity, innovation, psychological safety, trust, conflict resolution, resilience, and leadership skills. Talk about benefits!

Most emotionally intelligent people are often the smartest ones in the room, regardless of IQ or technical knowledge. They're the ones who remain calm when disaster strikes and make thoughtful decisions when facing stressful situations. They stand out like lighthouses in a storm, guiding the crew to shore.

Imagine having a team where every person is emotionally intelligent. They won't behave identically, but they'll be the type of people you can count on, and they'll form stronger connections.

Your Brain on Connection

Here's a neurological breakdown of what happens when teams connect versus when they struggle:

When people feel psychologically safe and connected, their brains release oxytocin, the trust hormone I mentioned in Chapter 1.[10] Oxytocin makes people more collaborative, productive, creative, and in tune with social cues.[11] It also keeps the prefrontal cortex—responsible for complex thinking—engaged.

When people feel excluded or threatened, their amygdala—the brain's alarm system—takes over in what's called "emotional hijacking." Rational thinking gets replaced by the fight-or-flight response.

This happens quickly in groups. When people feel happy and motivated, that positive emotional state spreads like wildfire—high morale, stronger connections, improved productivity. But when one or two people feel hostile, angry, or down, it spreads just as fast and tanks the entire group's vibe and performance.

The Play Advantage

Here, the topic of play becomes crucial for this discussion about brain chemistry. As I explained in Chapter 1, several things happen when people engage in play together:

- Brains release dopamine, enhancing learning and memory[12]
- Shared laughter triggers oxytocin release, creating social bonds[13]
- Activity and novelty stimulate neuroplasticity, rewiring the brain for better collaboration[14]

Despite rapid advances in brain research, with new and insightful studies published in respected medical journals every week, most scientists agree that we're still in the early stages of understanding how our brains work.[15] But here's what we do know: play activates multiple neural networks at once in ways that traditional (boring) team activities simply can't match.

Emotional Dynamics in Teams

Team emotional dynamics are far more complex and challenging to manage than individual emotions. Leaders aren't just working with each person's emotional state—they're managing the emotional climate of the entire group.

Each person brings different experiences, resources, likes, dislikes, biases, and emotional triggers. Tyler recognizes this complexity: "Workplaces today are full of different people. It's a multigenerational management mashup! Trying to decode and connect a team can feel like connecting a butter churn to OpenAI and asking it to make toast while walking your dog."

The best solution is often to approach this like a good teacher—take time to identify how each person learns and what they need to thrive, and then make sure you can accommodate everyone. It's more difficult than making a one-size-fits-all plan work, but it's much more effective.

Once you've learned about your team through observation and conversation, you can use a variety of team building programs to create authentic, relevant, and motivating activities that get lasting results from every single person.

Honoring how each person learns and thrives makes them more likely to feel safe, respected, and included. They'll be more likely to get involved, have fun, let loose, be open, and form bonds during activities. And that translates to better office dynamics and higher productivity.

What Are Emotional Triggers?

Triggers are stimuli that can cause automatic responses. They're essential when navigating mental health,[16] and since belonging ties into that, it's important to have a base understanding of them.

Triggers can be *anything*: certain phrases, tones of voice, news of failure, or even being paired with particular colleagues.

While it's not the leader's responsibility to help anyone work through their triggers (people spend years in therapy for this), it's helpful to recognize and respect them. The key is communication. When you have strong relationships, you can ask what motivates people and what their emotional triggers are. If people trust you enough to be honest, you'll learn invaluable information about what makes them tick and how to improve the emotional dynamics within your group.

For example, suppose one member has severe trust issues that surface on new projects. You talk to them, listen, and learn that they're prone to a fear of judgment when starting a big project.

With this information and what you know of the neuroscience of connection, you might introduce team building exercises that will release oxytocin to mitigate this. I've seen laughter yoga, improv workshops, empathy training, and even escape rooms work wonders this way.

That's how it's done!

The Results Are Worth It

Does this sound like hard work? It is!

It's not easy to keep connection, collaboration, neuroscience, and emotional intelligence in mind as a leader. It requires attention, empathy, and dedication, but it pays off by simplifying everything else.

You're not awake at night thinking, "How the *H-E Double Hockey Sticks* do I help them with their trust issues?! I'm not equipped for this!" Instead, you *are* equipped for it, and you can problem-solve before it ever keeps you up at night. It's easy to draw a connection between trust issues and the trust hormone when you think in terms of neuroscience, and it puts a lot of leadership stress on easy mode. It's true mastery of leadership on a social level.

Why Leaders Resist This Science

Leaders who only focus on technical skills and numbers often resist or dismiss discussions about emotions and connection. I get through to these folks by grounding everything in neuroscience, because of neuroscience.

I'm essentially taking Tyler's approach with teams and applying it to leaders. If a leader learns and thrives on numbers, I make my case with statistics and science. More often than not, this approach makes them realize why they can't sweep this under the rug.

Show them this is a competitive advantage they can't afford to ignore, back it up with proven research instead of feelings, and sell them on tangible benefits to their bottom line.

The Art of Building an Emotional Foundation

The beautiful thing about emotional intelligence and genuine connection is that these are learnable skills. Our brains remain adaptable throughout our lives—neuroplasticity is something you can tap into when you get your teams engaged with play and curiosity.

You don't achieve psychological safety with lectures, foster belonging with a company newsletter, or help a team bond through endless pointless meetings. You do these things with shared experiences that help people connect, trust, and become more emotionally intelligent so they can truly thrive.

The leaders who understand the neuroscience of connection can use this knowledge to hack their team dynamics and carve a pathway toward success and productivity. This leaves your competition in the dust, thinking, "Wait, what just happened, and how do I get *those* results?"

Play activates the right brain. Psychological safety unlocks potential. Belonging drives performance. Emotional intelligence amplifies everything. You now understand the psychology and neuroscience of gaining a competitive advantage.

When you understand human connection from this perspective, you can stop leaving brain chemistry to chance. No more throwing your hands up because you don't know what to do. Now you can begin creating the conditions that naturally foster a beautiful, sustainable web of connection between team members.

And this is only the beginning.

Now you need the tools and strategies to go from knowledge to measurable results, from theory to practice, and from engagement to impact. That, my friends, is exactly what we're exploring next.

CHAPTER 3

From Engagement to Impact

Twenty-five years ago, I was running events in my basement, convinced that the "power of play" was more than just a nice idea.

Today, TeamBonding has been named in the Inc. 5,000 list of fastest-growing companies multiple times, and we've worked with more than 7,000 companies so far. But the real lesson wasn't in the growth, but in discovering what moves the needle for team performance.

Here's what I learned: engagement gets people to show up and participate, and impact follows when those same people choose to stay, excel, and become the foundation of your competitive advantage.

Companies that truly get this difference don't throw simple pizza parties and force some lukewarm icebreakers into meetings to check boxes. These companies go out of their way to engage every single employee on their level. They're the ones creating cultures that give their top talent everything they need to thrive, and in turn, cultivate environments where these employees actually *want* to build their careers. These environments make every team member feel genuinely valued, and as a result, these companies turn long-term retention into a strategic advantage rather than an HR challenge.

"If we authentically put people first, the occupational outcomes and strategy will follow," adds Tyler. "People build the vehicles that get things done. So yes, engagement is a valuable measure, but generating impact inside teams creates fans for life."

Retain, Reward, Recognize

Let me tell you about Olivia, a marketing manager at a mid-sized software company. A brilliant natural leader, the type a business owner might build their organization's future around. Her manager thought he was doing everything right: competitive salary, good benefits, annual reviews that praised her work with zero critique.

He was shocked when Olivia quietly submitted her resignation letter at the beginning of the year.

Her exit interview revealed that she felt "invisible" and like she was "just another cog." This left her manager confused, too stunned to say anything. He'd given her everything she *needed*, but he'd missed what she *valued*: engagement, meaningful rewards, interest in her future, and recognition.

Now, retaining top talent is challenging—it demands ongoing effort. The job market is forever becoming more competitive, which means companies face ever-rising risk of losing valuable employees to rivals offering better salaries and benefits. The ability to retain employees like Olivia depends on their values and how they fit your company's culture, not just on their pay and benefits.

Keeping your highest-value employees is vital and replacing them is costly and time-consuming. Your top talent ensures your company achieves its goals, and without them, you'll likely start to sink.

But most business owners miss a crucial piece of this puzzle: every single person at your company is a high-value employee.

Value, Reward, and Recognize Everyone

Every member of your staff should receive the recognition and attention you'd give to your best employees. Here's why:

- **You never know who's a diamond in the rough:** Some people have the potential to become fantastic leaders, but they've shut down and accepted the grind after weathering monotony with other companies. Give them the same chances that a "high-value employee" would receive, and you might discover invaluable potential.

◆ **Happy employees improve retention rates and reputation:** I mentioned this in Chapter 2 while making a case for belonging—happy employees are more productive and innovative than unhappy ones, and they'll improve your company's reputation among potential talent and customers alike.

◆ **Culture is contagious:** When you treat your employees with equal respect, recognition, and opportunity, you build a culture that supports growth. Your company becomes more attractive, resilient, and profitable, setting the tone for long-term success.

When I say to treat your employees well, I mean **all** of them, including your interns—especially because companies are often dismissive of them. Interns represent future employees, brand advocates, and leaders. When you praise and recognize them, you reinforce a culture that values *everyone*.

About 60% of interns are offered full-time positions after completing their internships.[1] It's a good number, but I think it could be higher if more companies treated interns as more than an afterthought and considered their potential.

A Note on National Intern Day

If you've been ignoring interns, this is for you. When was the last time you celebrated National Intern Day, which is on the last Thursday of July? I don't mean buying a few pizzas and calling it a party. I mean, actually celebrating them in a meaningful way they'll be talking about for months (or years) to come.

As a leader, it's important to pay attention to the little things, and this is a prime example. National Intern Day is a golden opportunity to thank these up-and-comers for their fresh ideas, extra hands, and tech fluency. Give them public praise on social media, during meetings, and in your company newsletter. Get them face time with the higher-ups to open the door to future opportunities. Include them in team building events. Give them fun awards and titles.

All of these actions help interns feel genuinely part of your company and on even footing with your employees. You're not taking care of **everyone** if you're excluding your interns.

Don't Forget Remote Team Members

Another point to drive home: treating **all** your staff like top employees means recognizing your remote team members, too! Companies often forget about remote employees—a huge oversight that does you zero favors.

If an employee isn't happy with their current employer, there are plenty of fish in the proverbial sea. Remote workers are fishing from a much bigger sea, so making them feel valued is even more critical. Be appreciative and grateful to the people working from home, no matter where they are.

Pick team building events that remote team members can fully participate in and provide a remote-first company culture, or at least provide flexibility for any team members who would prefer to work from home.

Focusing on flexible, remote-first policies is just one of many ways you can improve employee engagement through your company culture.

Create a Culture of Employee Recognition and Happiness

A 2024 study by Gallup found that well-recognized employees are 45% less likely to have changed organizations in the last two years.[2] Younger generations especially want to work for companies that actively appreciate and recognize their contributions. And rightfully so.

Many leaders mistakenly fear that employee appreciation will strain their budgets, but lower turnover rates translate into higher profits. You'll spend more on recruitment, onboarding, and training new staff than you will on fostering a good company culture. You face lost productivity and opportunities every time you lose a team member. So, focus on retaining and training your current team instead of cutting corners.

It's all about creating a culture of employee recognition that makes team members happier, boosts morale, and improves engagement. This holistic approach can benefit every organization, yet so many still take an approach focused on short-term profits and productivity.

Team building events are a great option to build a healthier company culture, but it doesn't stop there. There are so many ways you can support your staff, and when you realize how much untapped potential you're sitting on, how could you not be inspired to implement these methods:

- ◆ **Be Open:** Excellent communication is a potent form of employee appreciation. Make frequent check-ins with every team member. Ask how their work is going, what challenges they're facing, and how you can provide better support. By genuinely listening and tending to their needs, you're fostering trust and loyalty in big ways. Most employees feel ecstatic when their boss implements a suggestion or responds to a request, and that's a feeling that pays dividends.
- ◆ **Be Genuine:** Nothing drives people away faster than feeling patronized. No one should tolerate this treatment, which is why leaders should always be genuine and honest. When you ask questions, really listen. Remember details about your staff, follow up with them, and never treat connection like a chore. If team members view you as a friend, they're less likely to jump ship.
- ◆ **Be Flexible:** I'll say it again because it's relevant in our post-lockdown society—employees want flexible work environments and schedules. They value companies that let them choose between remote and on-site work. Don't dictate terms; work with your team to find a solution that benefits everyone. People tend to deliver higher-quality results when they can choose where and even when they work.
- ◆ **Be Fun:** Sometimes your team needs to put away work and have some fun while they're on the clock. Show appreciation for their hard work by making time for breaks during work hours and planning team building events so they can let loose and have fun together.

The Four Non-Negotiables of Lasting Impact

Ah, the million-dollar question: What do employees want?

Let's take a quick look at the non-negotiables that create engagement and foster the kind of loyalty and performance that transforms businesses. It's what separates average companies from those with employees who drive real impact, and you wouldn't believe the amount of pushback I encounter when discussing the importance of meeting these needs with some business owners.

When this happens, I always remind them that failing to provide these benefits means they'll lose employees to competitors who do.

I've had to say it countless times: a company isn't losing out when it makes these changes. When you fulfill these non-negotiables, your bottom line benefits from happier employees who stay longer, perform better, and attract other high-quality talent.

Non-Negotiable #1: Fair Compensation and Benefits as the Foundation

Competitive pay and benefits aren't what create impact, but they *are* required to enable it. You can't build a high-performance culture on a wobbly foundation when your people deal with financial stress.

Trust me, when employees don't have to worry about making rent or covering healthcare, they suddenly have the energy to focus on excellence instead of survival.

You don't have to pay the highest salaries in your industry, but nothing else matters until you provide compensation that allows people to live comfortably. No one can bring their best selves to work when they're worried about money, and it's the only way to build a solid foundation that lets the real drivers of impact function.

Strong workplace relationships don't matter if you can't cover rent and other essential bills. Job stability isn't compelling if you don't make enough to pay for emergency expenses. Recognition is meaningless if money's so tight you can't enjoy life and destress sometimes. Insurance is pointless if it barely covers the basics.

So, pay your employees competitive rates and provide good benefits packages. If you don't, someone else will.

I could rattle off tons of stats here, but I don't need to. Just ask yourself this: if you were working day in and day out but your pay was so low that you struggled to make ends meet and take care of yourself, let alone enjoy life a bit, would you be happy?

If you think you'd be perfectly content or that this only happens when people "don't budget," you've forgotten what real struggle feels like.

If you were in this situation and came across a company offering a salary that allowed you to live comfortably, you'd take it no matter how many team building events your current company hosts.

Still not convinced? Look up the average overall expenses in your city per month. The numbers will vary from place to place, but they're often much higher than employers are willing to pay. Don't rationalize things like whether your team members should live with roommates to save on rent—start paying them enough that they don't have to make sacrifices just to get by.

The bottom line is that employers must meet the financial demands of their employees, even if it means lower profits in the short-term. They must provide in-demand benefits like health insurance, paid time off, retirement benefits, vision and dental insurance, parental leave, life insurance, HSA and FSA accounts, and 401(k) matching. Ideally, they should also consider other benefits employees appreciate, such as debt-repayment assistance, continuing education, mental health support, and professional development.

Non-Negotiable #2: Work-Life Balance as the Support Structure

Once you provide a solid foundation with fair compensation and good benefits, it's time to address work-life balance. This is your support structure. It's not just about making employees happy; focusing on work-life balance creates the conditions for sustainable high performance.

What's the point of good pay if you don't have time to enjoy life? Burnt-out employees don't drive innovation because they've run out of energy to go the extra mile. They're reduced to showing up, doing the minimum, and leaving so they can do it all again tomorrow.

Employees who have an actual work-life balance have the energy to bring creativity and focus to the office, and that's the gold that benefits your bottom line.

Here's what you should be offering if you want employees who create lasting impact:

- **Better Options:** I'll say it again, provide flexible remote and hybrid options. It boosts engagement and loyalty.
- **Better Hours:** Focus on output instead of hours. This shows your team members that you trust them to manage their schedules, and it nurtures people to take ownership of their work rather than just putting in time.
- **Better Time Off:** Provide generous paid time off so your team members can recharge. This helps avoid burnout while making your benefits package look stellar.
- **Better Schedules:** Many companies have moved to four-day workweeks, and they're seeing increased employee loyalty, trust, performance, and productivity as a result.

If someone you loved dearly said that they could switch employers and get more time off, shorter workweeks, and better flexibility with the same pay, you'd tell them to go for it! Your staff will find themselves in this situation when your competitors offer these benefits and you don't. And when they do, someone who loves them will tell them to go for it.

Non-Negotiable #3: Growth Opportunities to Create Mutual Value

Another reason employees leave good companies is when they find a better position with room for advancement. You can counter this by providing every employee with a clear path to help them move up the ranks, learn new skills, and advance their careers. This makes it clear that they're in a mutually-beneficial arrangement with your company, and that you see great value in them.

Ideally, you've already given them a solid foundation (good pay and benefits) and support structure (good work-life balance), so you'll be joining the ranks of legendary employers when you also give them good opportunities to grow.

No one wants to be in a dead-end job, but plenty of people get *stuck* in them. Don't be the place where people feel stuck—that's for mud, quicksand, and traffic jams. Not amazing workplaces. Be the garden where they can expand their roots and grow.

When you invest in your staff's professional development, you're simultaneously claiming your company's competitive edge. The following are examples of how you can do this for your team:

- Promote from within
- Provide paid training, classes, and skill-sharing workshops
- Pay for further education
- Offer mentorship programs and job shadowing
- Provide leadership development programs
- Create cross-training opportunities
- Schedule regular team building events that focus on skill development

Trust me, taking the time and effort to help your employees grow pays dividends later. How could you argue with better talent at your company? This is a big part of how I've built such a sustainable culture at TeamBonding.

One of Tyler's favorite techniques takes this even further. "I often tell managers to hold 'stay interviews,' not 'exit interviews,'" he explains. "They meet with each of their employees to find out what they like, what inspires them, favorite activities, what they want to do more of, why they like the company, and so on. This uncovers the individual algorithm of the employee that keeps them thriving. Then, you can right-fit reward, recognition, and appreciation tactics so they align with the individual. It's individualized management."

This approach moves management from a generic set of actions into something more personal, and it's ultimately better for everyone because it helps people get what matters most to each of them.

Non-Negotiable #4: Purpose-Driven Culture to Inspire Excellence

Let's circle back around to company culture because this is so important that I highlighted it before the non-negotiables. When employees feel connected to purpose, valued by leadership, and part of a company culture they enjoy, they step up.

Fostering a supportive and inclusive workplace isn't just about avoiding toxicity. Toxicity is a side effect of a bad environment. To create a culture you can be proud of, you need to provide an environment where people can do their best work. This means:

- **Hire and promote leaders** who value employee input and set a good example.
- **Create and maintain clear communication** channels and transparent decision-making processes.
- **Provide regular recognition** to connect individual effort to collective success.
- **Build more trust and psychological safety** by cultivating a genuine care for people at all levels.

We've already discussed each of these points in Part I because I'm passionate about them. I've created countless team building activities to help with all of this—programs designed to build trust, improve communication, and foster the bonds that make everything else easier. And I keep building them and stressing these points because they work.

How to Create Purpose-Driven Cultures

Here's a story that changed how I think about purpose. We were working with a healthcare system, and employee engagement scores were tanking. Turnover was high, morale was low, and management was convinced they needed "fun" activities to boost spirits.

But our needs assessment uncovered something interesting: the employees weren't burned out because they didn't like their jobs. These poor people were exhausted because they'd lost connection to their purpose. They got so wrapped up in metrics and compliance that they lost their passion for their industry.

So, we designed an experience that provided a stage for team members to share stories about patients whose lives they'd touched, colleagues who'd supported them, and moments when they knew they made a difference. There wasn't a dry eye in the room at the end of that event.

Six months later, their engagement scores were on the upswing, all because they had a chance to reconnect with their purpose.

When I shared this story with Tyler, he returned with his insight on it, saying, "I've learned that you can't just decide *to motivate* someone. But people can *be motivated*. Not by you, but by what sparks their passion! If you tap into a reason strong enough, something the entire team finds purpose in, those people will tear down walls to claim it."

One of Tyler's favorite ways to do this is through an art activity that prompts team members to paint a picture that answers a core question, like "What's your emotional connection to this job?" Once they've finished their paintings, they explain their answers one at a time before discussing how all their pieces come together to make a larger picture of what the team does. Next, they literally screw all the paintings together to create a massive mural for the office—a tangible reminder of their *why* as a team.

From Quiet Quitting to Quiet Thriving

Today's working world is plagued by a crisis of meaning, which is a major reason why purpose-driven cultures are so essential for engagement and impact. You've probably heard the term "quiet quitting"—it refers to doing the bare minimum of your job description, and it's shorthand for a widespread disengagement issue.

But there's an emerging counter-movement, "quiet thriving," and it's a beautiful thing. It's the difference between finding happiness in a meaningful role at a purpose-driven company and enduring your job because you have to. The quiet-thriving mindset is all about:

◆ Setting boundaries that preserve well-being
◆ Taking time to connect with colleagues
◆ Appreciating aspects of your work that energize you
◆ Looking for ways to make a difference

Employees who are quiet-thriving often aren't even aware they're doing it. They're simply working with companies that foster purpose-driven cultures, led by people who understand that a positive company culture is essential. If you're restructuring your company culture for engagement and impact, make it your goal to create a workplace of quiet-thriving people who'd never relate to quiet quitting.

The Four Pillars of Meaningful Work

Ready to create a purposeful workplace full of quiet-thriving people? I've identified four integral things to do just that after spending years perfecting the method at TeamBonding and reflecting on decades of experience. It's a short and sweet list, but you need each pillar to create the type of workplace I've been talking about throughout this chapter.

Pillar #1. The "Why" Behind Everything

This is bigger than a mission statement on the wall. It's the social purpose—the *reason* your company exists. It should be:

- ◆ Woven into daily operations and decision-making
- ◆ Connected to causes that matter beyond profit
- ◆ A source of pride for employees at every level

When your company demonstrates a commitment to authentic social purpose, when you have a *why* behind everything you do, you'll effortlessly drive both employee engagement and business success.

Pillar #2. Clear Value Alignment

Your employees should understand and feel appreciated for exactly how and why their individual roles help you create something bigger and work toward your company's purpose. When people see the impact they're making, work becomes meaningful.

For example, the secretary at a plumbing company should know she isn't just scheduling appointments; she's the voice of hope for stressed customers whose lives are on hold due to an emergency, and she's the first step in solving their problems.

Pillar #3. Opportunities for Growth and Connection

Regardless of industry, a workplace that gives employees a sense of purpose and happiness requires:

- ◆ Professional development that builds confidence
- ◆ Recognition that makes people feel valued
- ◆ Autonomy to take ownership of outcomes
- ◆ Relationships that create psychological safety

This is why even well-intentioned leaders can inadvertently drain meaning from work through practices that contradict these qualities. Setting unrealistic expectations, ineffective communication, and neglecting their employees can kill a team's purpose or drive.

Pillar #4. Social Impact

Today's employees, especially younger generations, seek out companies that make a difference. When you integrate social responsibility into your company culture, you'll start to see:

+ Higher employee engagement and retention
+ Stronger brand reputation and customer loyalty
+ Increased innovation and creativity
+ Better financial performance over time

You'll see its importance in Chapter 8, but it's the secret ingredient that combines work and purpose, creating something meaningful and worthwhile for everyone involved.

It's the Impact and Transformation That Matters

The goal of everything here—engagement, impact, value, purpose—is more than making people happy at work. We're creating conditions where people can do their best work and build skills that make everything easier for everyone, including your company.

Once you've witnessed the impact of engaging your team, giving them opportunities to connect, and building a workplace where every person is valued equally, you'll never want to go back. Your employees will solve problems faster, think more creatively, and support each other through every challenge. Your company will attract and retain top talent, and you'll see the benefits of doing so reflected in your bottom line.

If you want your business to thrive, giving your team all of this is non-negotiable. You should be asking yourself, "Can my bottom line afford to ignore the benefits of creating a thriving company culture?"

And the answer should be: No, it can't.

Tyler knows when engagement has truly transformed into impact: "Post-event, there's a tangible energy in the room. How people connect after programs. How people become accountable to each other and their work." That shift from going through the motions to genuinely caring is what separates companies that retain talent from those that constantly recruit it.

Everything in your business depends on your employees, and people perform best when they're connected, valued, and part of something meaningful. The science of connection, the power of play, and the strategies for engagement we've explored in Part I give you the foundation—next, it's time to learn how to design the moments that bring it all together and make these changes stick.

PART II

The Art of Designing Team Moments

The difference between team building events that transform organizations and those that make people roll their eyes lies in everything that happens before people even walk into the room.

Effective team building doesn't just happen, no matter how many executives think it should. If you skip the whole book, open Part III, pick an activity, and then throw your team into a room after barking the instructions at them, you'll get nowhere.

People actually do this, though, because it's all too easy to assume that magic happens naturally when it actually takes careful planning and intentional execution. It always reminds me of "Nailed It!"—it's a show where amateur cooks try to recreate beautiful, viral cakes and end up with hilariously bad results.

This Part isn't about my love of game shows, but about what I've learned over the years about everything that goes into team building when it works. It focuses on the framework I use to create transformational experiences, from understanding what your team actually needs to designing activities that deliver lasting results.

The Power of Intentionality

Before I get into the details, I want to share another story with you. This time, I was working with a Fortune 500 company that had a badly fractured leadership team following a massive internal restructuring and numerous layoffs.

Trust was at an all-time low with stakeholders and employees alike, and the CEO desperately told me, "I need an event to fix my teams. I don't know what's wrong with them!"

They'd worked with other team building companies that brought in generic events, read off instructions, and hoped for the best. These attempts actually set the company back when some employees submitted complaints about them. Still, a stakeholder recommended TeamBonding, and the CEO decided to give it one last shot.

I scheduled meetings with the company's CEO, the five department heads, and over a dozen front-line employees over three weeks. I asked about communication patterns, who trusted whom, what had changed since the layoffs, and what people were afraid to say out loud.

One pattern emerged: people felt blindsided. No one had explained the "why" behind the restructuring and layoffs, and rumors filled the vacuum. Trust hadn't eroded—it shattered.

So we designed a custom program built around rebuilding trust through structured vulnerability. We started with low-stakes activities where people could safely share frustrations without fear of judgment. Then we moved to collaborative problem-solving challenges that required different departments to depend on each other—the people who'd stopped talking now had to communicate to succeed.

We planned every transition, we put thought into every debrief question, and left nothing to chance. This was a huge job and, more than that, I'd grown to deeply care about the employees I spoke with.

Six months later, the company had its best quarterly performance in three years, stakeholders were thrilled, and the CEO called me wanting more.

Now, years later, this company runs quarterly team building sessions, its leaders implemented practices I've highlighted throughout the book, and they've maintained their improved performance, Glassdoor nearly doubled, and voluntary turnover dropped by 40% because they focused on building a culture where people actually want to work.

It all started with a carefully planned event that took everything into account and serious intentionality.

Transformation doesn't happen by accident. The activities themselves are just vehicles. The magic happens when you understand what a team actually needs, create the conditions for connection, and build experiences that unlock potential.

That company's transformation illustrates exactly what Part II is all about: the design that makes the difference.

What You'll Discover in Part II

- ◆ **Chapter 4: Start Smart Before the Event**—Learn how to assess team needs, secure leadership buy-in, and prepare your team for success with an upcoming event before setting the stage for action. This is where you build the foundation that makes everything else possible.
- ◆ **Chapter 5: Designing with Intention**—Discover the three-part architecture of transformational team experiences: foundation, structure, and atmosphere. Learn how to customize events based on your goals, your team's working situation, and everyone's personalities before looking at how to make every event an inclusive, safe space where real connection can happen.

Meet Your Guide: Paul Giroux

To bring you the best insights for this section, I tapped someone who understands these topics inside and out: Paul Giroux, TeamBonding's Director of Facilitator Training.

Paul brings more than two decades and over a million miles traveled as a facilitator, and he's refined the systems that transform events into repeatable success. He understands what makes events work consistently across different teams, industries, and challenges. His strategic thinking has been instrumental in helping TeamBonding grow, he's seen what separates the good from the great, and he knows how to translate that into practical frameworks that anyone can use.

As Paul puts it: "Our job is to give every participant an experience where they can interact with their coworkers, see them in a different light, and really feel part of something."

His insights throughout these chapters will help you understand that transformation happens when you create the right conditions for connection.

From Theory to Practice

The chapters ahead aren't about theory—they're about the practical frameworks that separate transformational events from forgettable ones. By the time you finish Part II, you'll know exactly how to assess what your team needs, design experiences with intention, and create the conditions where real breakthroughs can happen.

Let's get started.

CHAPTER 4

Start Smart Before the Event

I used to think preparing for a successful team building event meant having enough supplies and a Plan B for bad weather. Luckily, I was wrong. While supplies and backups do matter, they don't encompass what real preparation requires or why it can separate events that change teams from ones that waste time.

This was a hard lesson learned during an early event with a big corporate client. Everything that could go wrong did as soon as I arrived at the venue. The room I reserved was half the size I'd been promised. Then our materials arrived late, and the projector didn't work. It was a logistical disaster that left me feeling defeated before we even began, and my facilitators were as worried as I was. It felt like a bad dream where you show up to work with no pants on, and it took a lot of belief to move ahead anyway.

When the client's team arrived, we got raised eyebrows while we were running around putting out fires. But the whole thing turned out to be a massive success. Why? Because I'd spent hours understanding the leader's goals, who the team was, and what they needed. I'd already won without realizing it.

Once I did what I could for each issue at the venue, my facilitators and I had a huddle to discuss the team's goals. I'd taken detailed notes and given everyone a copy. Without the space and materials we'd expected, we improvised, turning my notes into our new plan.

I honestly didn't think it'd work. But I put on my best stand-up routine, diffused the tension with humor, and tried not to think about how the client's team probably knew things were falling apart. And you know what? I'm sure they did—but it didn't matter, because it became the experience the team needed to connect, and they focused on the results.

That day taught me that logistics matter more to the facilitators than the team. What matters to the team and its leader is results—whether you understand their goals and create an experience that addresses them. Participants will notice the facilitator more than the projector or room size, especially if you're surrounded by good people having good fun.

Do you understand the issue the team is having? Can everyone have fun with your activities? Do interactions feel natural instead of forced? These are the pieces that build the web of connection we've been talking about. I think of it like time with friends. What you're doing and where you are matters a little, but the main thing is who you're with and how you're connecting.

Of course, things go more smoothly when the room is big enough, the equipment works, and logistics aren't a mess. And yes, we've developed a formula to minimize these issues. But the human element matters most—and requires the most planning.

Paul Giroux, my close friend and Director of Facilitator Training, put it perfectly: "You're being judged from the moment their eyes hit the room. How you show up matters."

If you did well with everything leading to the start of an event—prior conversations, decisions about format and activities, the intention behind every detail—all that's left is to walk up and own the experience.

Paul is incredibly skilled at connecting with people in this way. He's taught our facilitators so much about how to capture attention, see the people in front of them, and connect with them in ways that keep them engaged and happy.

To do this, you must understand not only your audience but also their attention spans.

The Three-Minute Rule (And Why It's Getting Shorter)

Attention spans have changed dramatically since I started this business. They're shrinking faster every year, and this directly impacts the human side of team building.

"Phones and TikTok and everything have really shortened attention spans," says Paul. "From a facilitating standpoint, you have to be more on your toes. Pre-pandemic, you had five minutes to capture a room. Post-pandemic, you have three. If you can't get engagement up in the first three minutes, people start looking at their screens."

Three minutes. That's how long you have to prove you're not wasting their time. No pressure, right?

The good news is that it isn't just what you say in those three minutes. People also notice your energy. If the vibe immediately says, "This is going to be different," they'll give you more credit. And if the facilitators are enthusiastic and energized and the room feels fresh, even better! You want to let participants know they're here for something interesting.

Don't get me wrong, what you say matters too. I've seen facilitators lose entire groups in 30 seconds by starting with a dry voice saying:

"Okay, everyone. Welcome. We're going to do some team building and trust exercises today."

Game over. You can almost *hear* the collective eye-roll. Unless something changes, it's all downhill from there.

Beyond What They Think They Want

Most leaders and team members don't know what will resolve the issues in the office. They often have an idea of the changes they want to see, but the gap between their vision and what their team's needs can be huge.

"It helps to start by describing what we do and what experiential team building is," says Paul. "I explain that our job is to come in and make sure every participant can enjoy a fun and vibrant program where they can interact with one another and start to see their coworkers and leaders in a different light. I also explain that we need to meet teams on their level based on their personalities, interests, and state of mind."

This step is crucial. Events rarely crash because of the content. It's usually a misalignment between expectations and reality. The leader needs to know why they're bringing us in, and I need to know what they want me to address.

The First Conversation

Once they have a better idea of what team building is about, it helps to ask them to explain their issue or list their goals. This usually gets the discussion started with answers like:

- ◆ "We need better communication. No one is on the same page, and they're not talking to each other like a team!"
- ◆ "We have certain people who don't communicate the way we want them to, and we don't like it. Also, our staff doesn't trust us!"

This gives us a starting point before we launch into the full discovery process.

The Discovery Process

Going through the discovery process with a team building client is similar to what doctors experience daily.

The initial questions above are sort of like the intake paperwork that people fill out after Googling their symptoms. Here, and in the initial conversations, they'll tell the doctor what they've diagnosed themselves with.

Then, the doctor uses this information as a starting point, asking questions to understand their symptoms and overall health from an expert's zoomed-out perspective.

Finally, the doctor takes a moment to look at the big picture before providing a diagnosis, which is usually different from what the patient expected, and often with a more straightforward solution.

We don't use a set of prescribed questions—the following are just examples. It's about having a genuine interaction and intuitively asking the right questions. If the first questions don't get results, move to different ones until you figure it out.

Example Question #1: "What's the problem and when did you notice it?"

This is one of the first things you need to know. It expands on the initial discussion. You need to learn what happened that helped the leader realize something needs to change.

When someone says they have an issue like "communication problems," dig deeper with questions like:

- What specific aspects of communication have broken down?
- When did the problems start?
- Are there specific individuals whose communication is lacking? Others who communicate well?
- What are some examples of how you became aware of these issues?

What they think is a communication problem might really be a trust issue, a lack of role clarity, or a leadership problem. Asking these questions helps me get a better perspective so I can start getting to the heart of things.

Example Question #2: "What's the team's energy like?"

Once you've asked enough questions to understand the issue, it's time to feel out the team's vibe if the first step didn't naturally lead me here.

You should be able to visualize their energy and who you're working with. This means asking more questions to understand the people on the team and the symptoms they're experiencing:

- How does the team talk about each other?
- Do you hear "we" language or "they" language?
- Do they seem energized by the prospect of working together, or resigned to it?

Ask for information about each team member, too:

- What do they enjoy?
- Why are they in this industry?
- How do they show up for work each day?
- Are there things they don't enjoy doing?
- What gets them excited?
- What do you overhear the team saying in hushed tones?

Energy tells you more than words, so pay close attention to these answers. Take notes throughout the process to create a picture of the team before designing the event.

Example Question #3: "What are their patterns like when they fail? When they succeed?"

Finally, after you really understand who you're working with and why, it's good to hear about the team's best and worst moments.

This helps you learn how they work as a task group—you want to know what worked when things went well, what didn't when things fell apart, and why these strategies were or weren't effective.

Use these answers to compile a list of examples and identify patterns that reveal two important things:

◆ Conditions that help this team thrive
◆ Conditions that should be avoided

Sometimes, asking the client about a pattern you've identified is helpful, but don't always take their word for it if they disagree. Ask why they disagree and explore their perspective further. They might be in denial or too focused on how they function as individuals rather than how their team works as a group.

Diagnosing the Issue

After asking the discovery questions, it's time to review the evidence and make a diagnosis based on the notes you've taken. Use the information you gathered to zoom out and get a clear perspective on the root issues.

If you can't find a clear diagnosis or if you need a bit more information, ask the client follow-up questions like these:

◆ **Connection gaps:** Is the issue that people don't know or trust each other?
◆ **Role confusion:** Are the team members dealing with unclear responsibilities or overlapping territories?
◆ **Process breakdown:** Is the real problem that the processes in place to complete work just aren't working?

- ◆ **Leadership vacuum:** Are team members struggling because they lack clear direction or decision-making authority?
- ◆ **Change fatigue:** Is there too much disruption without sufficient support in the company?

Reading Today's Teams

Something else has shifted in the last few years. Teams have different needs and perspectives than they did even five years ago.

"Today's best companies are in tune with making sure everyone's a part of their culture," agrees Paul. "You get more questions like, 'Is this inclusive?' 'Is it fair?' 'Is it something everyone can get behind?'"

These are the kinds of things leaders need to think about, and it's why DEIB is such a big deal. And sometimes, you'll find that the team's true issue is an outdated workplace, a lack of DEIB, or some other problem that needs to be addressed at the organizational level.

If you encounter a diagnosis like this, be honest with the client about your suspicions to whatever degree they're receptive. Talent is getting younger, the workforce is more diverse, and companies can't afford to fall behind if they want to attract and retain skilled employees.

When companies miss this, they're not just dealing with a few failed team building events—they'll start seeing talent walk out the door.

Leadership Buy-In: The Make-or-Break Factor

Before you can start reaping the rewards of team building, you need buy-in from the higher-ups. Take the Fortune 500 company I mentioned earlier. While I'm proud to have been part of their change, I can't take all the credit for the success they saw.

If upper management hadn't applied lessons from our events, the results wouldn't have stuck. Effort is required throughout the process—from the first talks to planning, execution, and follow-through—not just from me, but also from the company and its leadership.

Here's a scenario I see all the time: a well-meaning HR director books a team building event while the department head rolls their eyes and jokes about "trust falls and kumbaya." These events tend to have little lasting impact because the leaders aren't listening to the lessons, investing in sustained change, or communicating their goals to their teams.

Paul's approach to this challenge has evolved to address the disconnect with humor:

> "I'll tell groups how funny and interesting it is that, when I fly around the country doing all of these events, people always say, 'Oh my God, my company needs that!' But when I'm paid to be somewhere for a team building event, everyone immediately cringes or wants to be somewhere else, and leaders say something like, 'Oh no, we don't need this, what a waste of time.'"

By highlighting this, Paul gives people permission to be skeptical while opening the door for authentic engagement. And it works. It also highlights behavior leaders don't want to be guilty of. They've probably said how much they need team building and then knocked it when it was time to schedule it, and those statements help them recognize the fallacy in that reaction.

Securing real leadership buy-in takes more than addressing skepticism. It requires helping leaders understand precisely what they're investing in and why. "You've got to understand what led them to us and what their goals are," adds Paul. "Then look at the program and say, 'Okay, how do we deliver this to match what they're looking for?'"

This isn't about selling them on team building. It's about ensuring alignment between their needs and our approach. It's difficult for anyone to look at that kind of solution and decide they don't need it.

Preparing the Participants
Once you have leadership buy-in, involve them by discussing how to properly prepare participants. Their input helps each event have a

good chance of succeeding, not just in execution and reception, but in results. Here's what I usually recommend:

- **Set clear expectations:** Tell team members what to expect without ruining surprises. They need practical information about dress code, schedule, participation level, and anything they might want to bring. Get them hyped and help them understand this isn't a regular meeting.
- **Address skepticism early:** Acknowledge that some team members will be skeptical or hesitant to participate. Lots of people have had bad experiences with team building, and they deserve permission to participate at their comfort level. Encourage and reward engagement when they do jump in!
- **Create psychological safety:** Let people know they're going to make mistakes, that this is expected and encouraged, and that no one will judge them. Tell them that having fun while learning is the only goal, and that leaders are here to learn as equals.
- **Framing the purpose:** Explain why you're investing time in this and why everyone should care about the results. Connect the activities to tangible business outcomes, even if that's just a more laid-back culture and better DEIB. Discussing upskilling, destressing, and getting away from the day-to-day helps drum up excitement for team building.

Setting the Stage: Environment, Format, and Timing

I started this chapter with a story about an event in a room that was too small without the right supplies, but that doesn't mean I don't emphasize setting the literal stage for success. The physical environment isn't irrelevant, nor is it absolutely critical. It matters, just not always in the way you might expect.

I've my top facilitators pull off incredible events in impossible spaces. Paul, for example, once told me about running a program in a test kitchen in New York, saying it was "a shoebox of a room." The team struggled to even get a screen and projector into the space. Everyone was blown away that they successfully hosted the event there, and they received fantastic feedback afterward.

Paul likes to say our job is to work with what we have, wherever we are. Flexibility and adaptation are more important than perfect conditions. He calls his approach the *Dr. Seuss method* and puts it like this:

"On a plane, on a boat, on a train—I'll spark teamwork joy from Maine to Spain!"

Practical Environment Guidelines

Adaptability is non-negotiable. It's what puts the "extra" in extraordinary team building facilitators. That said, you also need to set people up for success, get the most practical environment possible, and ensure you get the most out of your space. That means understanding how your environment affects energy, connection, and engagement:

For High-Energy Events

Nothing kills enthusiasm faster than being stuck in a cramped space. It can work in some cases, but people need room to move, gesture, and feel physically free. If you're stuck with a small space, choose activities that work within those constraints or go outside and improvise. Otherwise, you'll be forcing square pegs into round holes.

For Intimate Conversations

Boardroom setups can work, but they need to encourage eye contact and human connection rather than reinforce hierarchy. I almost always remove the table and arrange chairs in a circle so everyone can sit and talk on a more human level, preventing anyone from slipping into meeting mode.

For Creative Collaboration

Flexible spaces that can be reconfigured are gold. People think differently when they can move around and interact with their environment. Ideally, have furniture you can move and open wall space for ideas. You can make it work outdoors or in less-than-ideal spaces by setting up your props, stations, seating, and anything else as though you're in a big room. Sometimes it helps to outline a rectangle during setup to visualize this.

For Virtual Events

Technology becomes your environment. Test everything twice, have backup plans, and remember that people's homes create a different kind of intimacy than office spaces. Treat it like setting up a physical space, and don't assume you can put in less effort.

How to Make a Good First Impression

Here are some factors I add to checklists for my teams to make sure that judgment works in our favor:

- ◆ **Visual Impact:** Does your room or setup tell a story people will be interested in? Make sure it says "something different is about to happen here" (not "welcome to another boring meeting"). Use distinctive, creative arrangements so participants can see, feel, and trust this won't be business as usual.
- ◆ **Audio Atmosphere:** Does your music set the right expectations? Choose music that matches your desired energy level, and consider asking leadership what genres the team likes if music is a big focus.
- ◆ **Material Presentation:** Are your supplies arranged thoughtfully? The way you present materials communicates your level of preparation and professionalism.
- ◆ **Facilitator Positioning:** Do you know where you and other facilitators will be when people enter the room? Make sure you're positioned confidently, ready to welcome them with your full attention.

Timing Considerations

It's essential to review some timing considerations before the event begins. This includes everything from the time of year to the start time.

Season and context matter. Anything happening in the organization or in people's lives at the time of the event will affect the energy and success. I try to avoid peak business periods, months with major deadlines, or times of year when people are already stressed, or at least work with it if it's unavoidable. The holidays are an exception—I don't entirely avoid them, but I lean into it so people can get into the spirit and celebrate at work.

The time of day has a huge impact. This is especially true during hot or cold seasons and for any outdoor event. If you're hosting a program with outdoor elements in summer in a hot city, schedule it for early morning or late afternoon to avoid the hottest hours. If it's winter, schedule outdoor activities during the sunniest parts of the day to keep moods high, and try to get patio heaters if possible.

Starting on time is crucial. No matter what time the event is scheduled for, always start on time. It shows respect for participants' time and sets a professional tone. That said, if people are coming from other meetings or a conference, I build in a short buffer so anyone running late has time to get there, and everyone else can wind down.

The duration matters too. Match the length to the energy requirements of the activities. High-intensity activities work best in short bursts. Longer events need varied pacing and natural breaks. End on time, especially if people are heading home afterward—sending people home late doesn't leave a good impression and can interfere with their plans.

Bringing It All Together

Preparation doesn't need grand theories—it needs clarity. Everything in this chapter has been about building the right foundation. Once you have that, there's no need to overcomplicate things. The heart of preparation is about understanding your people, your purpose, and your plan.

You need to understand what the team needs, read their energy, and secure genuine leadership buy-in to create a solid foundation.

Next, we'll look at how we design experiences with precision to meet each person and team where they are with what they need.

From there, the real art begins!

CHAPTER 5

Designing with Intention

I've had plenty of moments over the past couple of decades that highlight the difference between strategic team building and forced fun. One experience stands out.

A tech startup founder once called us in desperation, saying, "My team is falling apart! They're brilliant individually, and I hired them all for a reason, but they can't work together to save their lives . . . or my company. I need help fast."

During the discovery process, we learned that the issue wasn't a skills problem or a personality conflict. This was a group of introverted experts forced into intensive collaboration without preparation, trust, or strong bonds.

If we'd thrown them into high-energy games, everyone would've been miserable. Instead, we made a careful diagnosis and designed a custom-made event—a series of low-key, intellectually engaging challenges that let people contribute their strengths without forcing extroversion.

The transformation was remarkable. Eight months later, that same "falling apart" team had launched two successful products and voluntarily started having lunch together every Friday. They scheduled another low-key event to celebrate the second launch, ending with a relaxed happy hour. Before leaving, one team member asked about our other events, and the group got excited to try a scavenger hunt.

They went on to try several of our high-energy programs—the types of games that wouldn't have been the right choice in the beginning—and they loved them! This is why I emphasize meeting groups on their level. You can't apply generic solutions or prescribe the same event for every team. You have to understand what each team needs and customize experiences that work for them.

Through these experiences, we've developed an architecture for meaningful team experiences. Like any well-made building, it starts with a solid foundation, then a defined structure, and finally the finishing touches:

- **Foundation:** Examine the purpose. What specific outcome are you trying to achieve for the leader and participants? This goes deeper than vague goals like better communication and into real challenges and opportunities. It's what allows you to work at their level and get results.
- **Structure:** Consider the best activities for this group. What experiences will create the conditions for the outcome you're trying to achieve? This isn't just about the activities, but how you introduce them, transition between elements, and help the team process what they're learning. By giving structure extra care, you make it easier for the team to apply the lessons afterward.
- **Atmosphere:** Consider how to deliver the event. How will you create an environment where people feel safe to authentically engage? This includes the energy each facilitator brings and the implicit messages from leadership or ones you believe are necessary—especially around risk-taking and vulnerability.

When team building fails, it's often because it only focused on structure. The activities are important, but if you built a building like this, it'd fall apart without a foundation, and it wouldn't be livable without finishing touches.

Activities are just the vehicle. The transformation happens in the spaces between them. Those moments are when people see each other differently, which is especially important for teams like the one I mentioned, where brilliant introverts needed to learn to work together.

Customizing to Meet the Team's Needs

The discovery questions in Chapter 4 help us understand what leaders mean when they say things like "work together better." Your job doesn't end with the diagnosis from Chapter 4, though.

No, now it's time to figure out what to do about that diagnosis. Luckily, many team challenges fall into one of the following three categories, each requiring different approaches.

Common Issue #1: Connection—When People Don't Really Know Each Other

The most common issue teams face. It's part of why I landed on "TeamBonding" as my company's name. Connection-focused events are also my favorites because they address such an integral part of working on a team.

You can't effectively collaborate with people you don't know or trust unless everyone's already experienced with collaboration. Even then, bonding makes things better.

Connection-focused events are crucial for:

◆ New teams or teams with new members
◆ Remote teams that lack the casual "watercooler" interaction opportunities
◆ Teams that have been through significant change or conflict
◆ Groups where interpersonal relationships are purely transactional

Design Principles for Connection

Every team, company, and situation is unique, but I haven't spent time in this industry examining patterns for nothing. We've developed four principles that foster and reward genuine connections:

◆ **Start with lower-risk activities:** Lead with activities that feel safe, even for strangers, and gradually increase the vulnerability factor. For example, if you execute it well, starting with a "Two Truths and a Lie" icebreaker creates a more open energy than asking people to share deeply personal stories right away.

◆ **Create structured sharing experiences:** Design around the fact that connection is integral to being human. When someone wants to connect, they often don't know how, but team building provides frameworks for structured sharing. This gives people permission and guidelines for deeper conversations.

◆ **Include movement and shake it up:** Humans thrive on motion—it breaks down barriers faster than sitting still and helps people form bonds. Tap into it and use it to switch up the energy if it's low, even if you're just taking advantage of how effective walking meetings are.[1]

◆ **Add casual reflection time:** We'll get into debriefing later, but I usually suggest that teams plan time to enjoy a meal together after an event to make time for casual reflection. Everyone will naturally want to unwind and reflect when the activity is over, and this is connection gold. It also helps the lessons stick!

Honeybee: A Story of Connection

Paul told me about a powerful moment during a virtual onboarding program he facilitated for a group of hundreds of interns. He was running a high-energy virtual game show and asked everyone to stay engaged in chat, which became a vital ongoing conversation.

One participant—we'll call her Lilly—mentioned working with honeybees to help cure cancer, and Paul stopped everything to talk to her. He wanted to capture the moment and give everyone a chance to hear her story, so he asked her to unmute and tell him about her research and work using bee venom as an anti-cancer agent.

They returned to the game show soon enough, but he'd made room for a human moment while serving as a prime example of how to connect and let Lilly shine.

A few months later, at an in-person skateboard-building event for this company, someone suddenly said, "Oh my God, Paul! Paul! It's you! It's me, it's Honeybee!" And they connected again! Some of Lilly's peers joined in, and the conversation continued all the way to dinner! Now *that's* a good example of the power of connection.

Common Issue #2: Creativity—When Teams Are Stuck in Routine Thinking

A lack of creativity is a common complaint I hear from leaders. They've hired intelligent, creative people, and they're not getting the innovative results they expected. It's usually not about team members not being creative, but being stuck in a routine or in left-brain thinking. People crave fun and creative experiences, so you want activities that'll jumpstart right-brain thinking!

I'm fascinated by creativity and how the brain works when those right-brain gears start turning. It's a skill and a state of mind interwoven with leaps in human history. Just as necessity is the mother of invention, creativity is the toolbox people use to bring life to those inventions.

Much of my time has been spent developing creativity-focused programs alongside brilliant people who help make TeamBonding work. When we pour right-brain thinking into a new event, we help teams break patterns and find new ways to overcome challenges. They work well for:

- Teams facing new challenges that require innovative solutions
- Groups too comfortable with "how we've always done it"
- Organizations wanting to encourage more creative thinking across all roles
- Teams where some members don't see themselves as "creative types"

Most leaders think more freedom leads to better innovation, and while I support giving teams freedom, the opposite is often true here. Creativity flourishes within constraints. If you can throw any solution at the board, you won't get unexpected answers. When a team must find a solution that fits specific parameters and the answer is hard to find, their brains engage, and creativity comes into play.

We have a challenge called Product Pipeline that exemplifies this. Teams break into small groups and receive identical materials to meet specific build requirements. It's those requirements that force innovation. Constraints don't limit creativity—they channel it toward practical problem-solving while allowing for wildly different approaches.

Design Principles for Creativity

Trying to target something as ephemeral as creativity in a short program might seem overwhelming, but time constraints have helped me develop proven design principles. Here's a short rundown:

◆ **Embrace constraint:** Set specific parameters, then give team members freedom to find solutions within them. Unlimited resources and no rules usually produce less innovation. Just ensure multiple approaches can work.

◆ **Encourage rapid iteration:** Plan opportunities for teams to try multiple approaches quickly. This reduces pressure on any single idea, encourages experimentation, and prevents teams from locking onto the first answer they find. It's great for events and equally valuable for company projects.

◆ **Celebrate unexpected solutions:** Make space for ideas that seem "wrong" to help remove the fear of failure. When your team taps into creativity, celebrate it. Praise failures as stepping stones and honor the fact that innovative solutions often come from combining ideas in unexpected ways after learning from missteps.

Pro Tip: "Don't over-obsess and make everything too ruley," adds Paul. "Keep an open mind and focus on your big goals and where you need to be so your team can figure out how to get there together."

Common Issue #3: Collaboration—When Individual Stars Can't Become a Team

Collaboration is another common pain point. Many leaders don't realize it's a skill that requires practice, and generic team building activities often fail to teach it effectively.

Collaboration uses a completely different skillset than solo work, and if you don't give employees the chance to refine it, how can you expect them to master it?

These issues are rarely caused by people refusing to work together. More often, brilliant individuals who've thrived through self-reliance find that their usual approach of taking charge and powering through undermines the team's success. These high performers are often promoted because they can handle anything thrown at them. But once they're on a team, they miss the importance of slowing down, listening, and integrating others' ideas.

Collaboration-focused events work by addressing communication, decision-making, leveraging strengths, and managing the creative tension of multiple perspectives. They're often designed so that collaborating is the only path to success, and rightfully so.

Events like this tend to get great results for:

- ◆ Teams with strong individual performers who struggle to work together
- ◆ Groups with unclear roles or overlapping responsibilities
- ◆ Teams where some voices dominate while others aren't heard
- ◆ Organizations implementing new collaborative tools or processes

When I'm struggling to pinpoint the cause of a group issue, targeting collaboration is an effective diagnostic tool. It'll either confirm the problem or help uncover the real issue. And since these skills benefit from regular reinforcement, it's never a wasted effort.

Design Principles for Collaboration

Events focused on collaboration help people learn to work together effectively and discover that this can be easier, more efficient, and even fun. Once they experience this shift, people often seek out collaboration rather than dread it. I like to keep these design fundamentals in mind:

- ◆ **Make interdependence necessary:** Create challenges that require each person's strengths and contributions. Avoid anything where one or two people can carry the group, and lean into the idea that they'll fail without full participation. Demand genuine collaboration and make the reward exciting so everyone's eager to succeed.
- ◆ **Rotate leadership roles:** Create opportunities for everyone to step in and lead. This helps teams discover hidden leadership in quieter members, practice under different leadership styles, and let natural leaders refine their skills in new situations.
- ◆ **Include processing discussions:** Events should focus on more than the task, extending to conversations about how the team is working and what they could do differently. This isn't

just post-event—it should happen during the activity to teach and reinforce collaboration.

◆ **Create transparent decision points:** Include moments where teams must decide together and highlight them so everyone sees how decisions are made. This shines a light on unconscious collaboration problems, and as they troubleshoot what isn't working, they'll start trying to fix it.

Virtual, In-Person, and Hybrid: What Works Where

Today's corporate world offers a wide range of options for how and where people work. The WFH (work-from-home) crowd was already growing pre-pandemic, but lockdown forced many to expand their concept of an office environment. I learned so much about the strengths and limitations of virtual, in-person, and hybrid events.

I also changed as a person. Where I once preferred in-person meetings, I now enjoy video calls because I can spend time with people from around the world any day of the week. It even makes the obligatory weather questions more interesting because I get to hear what it's like in different states and countries!

Here's a quick tour of each format and some helpful considerations for making them work.

Virtual Events: The Surprising Depth

I'll admit that I didn't always believe in the power of virtual events, but after lockdown, I'm a convert.

"If you asked me prior to doing virtuals, I probably would've never said virtual events can be super impactful," Paul agrees. "But after leading so many of these online programs and meetings, I know they can be so impactful for everyone involved, and I love them!"

Virtual Strengths

◆ **Accessibility:** People can participate regardless of location or mobility constraints
◆ **Frequency:** Lower logistical barriers mean you can do shorter, more frequent sessions
◆ **Global reach:** Teams can include members from anywhere

◆ **Chat engagement:** Multiple conversation streams can happen simultaneously

◆ **Unexpected intimacy:** Seeing people in their home environments creates different, more personal connections

Virtual Design Considerations

◆ **Shorter attention windows:** Paul's three-minute rule is even more critical in virtual events, where people can covertly start scrolling

◆ **Chat moderation:** Active chat engagement is crucial for keeping everyone involved

◆ **Breakout strategy:** Smaller groups are more important for meaningful conversations and comfort

◆ **Technical backup plans:** Always have contingency plans for connectivity issues (like backup plans for bad weather)

Paul's favorite virtual event format is the game show because it creates natural energy and engagement, especially when you use the chat function to keep everyone participating simultaneously rather than waiting for turns to speak.

Virtual Event Technical Guidelines

This checklist can help keep the key technical aspects in mind when running any virtual event:

◆ **Platform selection:** Tech issues are annoying. Choose reliable platforms that support your group size and interaction needs. Test all features beforehand (twice), and do the same for a backup platform in case of issues.

◆ **Audio quality:** Poor audio kills engagement fast. Invest in good microphones and high-speed internet for facilitators—no one wants to hear broken-up audio for 90 minutes.

(continued)

- **Visual quality:** Poor video is another engagement killer. Use good cameras and lighting, position cameras at eye level, and avoid distracting backgrounds or use virtual ones with a proper green screen.
- **Ongoing engagement:** Static presentations don't work virtually. Use screen sharing, breakout rooms, and interactive tools. Show your face as the default and only turn off video when necessary.
- **Participation management:** Use polls, chat, and breakout rooms so everyone can contribute. Plan an interactive moment every 10 minutes to maintain attention.
- **Technical preparation:** Remember, test everything twice, have backup plans for connectivity issues, and always have a tech helper during events.

In-Person Events: The Irreplaceable Energy

Physical presence creates possibilities that virtual can't replicate. There's something unique about the energy of shared space, seeing full body language, and the absence of screen fatigue.

Humans have evolved to crave the company of others, and screens haven't been around long enough for our brains to adapt. Video calls offer benefits, but the brain responds more viscerally to someone ten feet away than to someone on a screen.

In-Person Strengths

- **Physical Movement:** Activities involving movement break down barriers faster
- **Nonverbal Communication:** Full body language provides richer information
- **Shared Experience:** Physical presence creates more vivid memories
- **Spontaneous Interaction:** Unplanned conversations during breaks often provide value
- **Sensory Engagement:** Touch, smell, and spatial awareness add richness to the experience

Paul's favorite in-person event, *In It to Win It*, exemplifies this. He told me he wouldn't mind doing that event every day for the rest of his life since the program combines physical challenges with team strategy.

Hybrid Events: The Complex Challenge

Hybrid events are the most complex. In these, some participants are in-person and others join virtually. This offers unique flexibility but also creates challenges and the risk of two-tiered experiences.

The approach Paul and I use prioritizes inclusion. If you're on-site with virtual participants, it's the facilitator's job to make the online members feel just as included as those in person.

"It's so much more important to constantly find ways to interact with those that are virtual so they can feel part of what's going on," adds Paul.

Hybrid Event Guidelines

In addition to following the in-person and virtual guidelines above, hybrid events require a few additional considerations. These are my top priorities when working on hybrid programs:

- **Dedicated virtual attention:** Have moments where you're exclusively addressing virtual participants. They should feel included and like they're receiving special attention, because they are!
- **Shared digital tools:** Use platforms both groups can access equally. Even better if there's a chat function and progress meters to encourage communication and real-time feedback.
- **Role rotation:** Give virtual participants leadership roles in several segments so they get the full experience and a chance to strengthen those muscles. You'll have natural leaders and quiet folks in both groups, and you don't want to gloss over your remote team members.
- **Technical support:** Have dedicated tech support to resolve any issues quickly. There's nothing worse than being on the other side of the screen while your in-person colleagues are having a great time and you're stuck troubleshooting or completely disconnected.

Of course, the experience between in-person and online members won't be identical, but that's not the goal. What you want is an equally valuable event for each group.

Think back to the image I used when defining equity in Chapter 2—you'll need to give your online participants a little boost, and that's what doing it right looks like.

Inclusion by Design: Creating Space for Every Voice

Regardless of which format you choose, one principle applies to all: creating moments where everyone feels safe to participate.

Inclusion requires balancing invitation with choice. You need to take the situation and setting into account so everyone feels welcome to engage while maintaining the option to participate at their comfort level.

Let's review the basics of intentional, inclusive event design to give a top-down view of the concept.

Inclusive Design Strategies

Intentional event design focuses on inclusion for all people without judgment of different personalities and preferences. It includes:

- **Open-ended questions:** Ask questions that allow everyone to answer at whatever level feels comfortable. For instance, "Tell us something interesting about yourself" allows for both surface-level and deeply personal responses, keeping the question inviting for all types.
- **Multiple participation channels:** Provide ways for people to contribute through speaking, writing, movement, or creative expression. This is especially true for virtual or hybrid formats, but it's also helpful for in-person events. I like to incorporate several roles for each member at every stage to make this happen.
- **Small group options:** Many people will share in groups of 3–4, even if they won't speak up in a large group. That's why I usually split larger teams into smaller groups. It gives extroverts enough people to enjoy team energy, while offering introverts a more comfortable setting to contribute.

- ◆ **Time to think:** Build in reflection time before asking for responses. Not everyone processes quickly, and some people need a few minutes to decide what to say. If a few minutes isn't feasible, they at least need a few seconds.
- ◆ **Anonymous options:** Sometimes, the best insights come when people don't have to put their name on ideas. This isn't relevant to every group, but it's appreciated more often than you'd think. Even talkative, extroverted people may jump at the chance to contribute anonymously because it removes fear of judgment and creates more psychological safety.

Reading Resistance vs. Discomfort

What appears to be resistance is often uncertainty about how to contribute. Creating clear, specific roles helps people find their place without forcing participation. Active resistance is rare unless the event feels like forced fun.

"When I find disinterested people at programs, generally I can just walk over with a smile and check in with them," says Paul. "That can diffuse the discomfort or reveal that they didn't feel like there was something they could do to help the team. You can't go wrong by talking to people and engaging them on a personal level with friendliness. If they're actively resisting, this same strategy helps you figure that out quickly, and then you can address it by understanding the source and responding appropriately."

Leadership's Role in Sustaining Change

Leaders who look at their teams and see things they want to change are the ones who most often seek out or plan team building events. They'll spend hours, days, weeks, and months thinking about what's wrong with their team, often without looking in the mirror long enough to see how their own behaviors might be impacting their crew.

This lack of self-reflection quickly undermines their ability to drive lasting change. After all, why would the staff keep doing something the leaders have given up on?

The way a team's leader behaves before, during, and after an event affects the outcomes and determines whether the lessons will stick. It's like the saying, "Whether you think you can, or you think you cannot, you're right."

The leaders who think team building will lead to lasting change, and those who believe it won't, are both usually correct. It's about the power of attitude and intention.

A leader who believes team building will create lasting change is more likely to apply the lessons and prompt their team members to do the same.

A leader who believes team building is just a pointless day off is less likely to adopt and model the behaviors they learned, and more likely to look for proof their team has forgotten the lessons.

Is this always true? Of course not. But in my experience, it's a pattern. Leaders need to walk the walk. Beyond applying new skills and lessons, they should focus on being open and emotionally vulnerable so they're a safe person for their team to make mistakes around.

As Paul put it, "Being open is not something you can turn on and turn off. You can't just be open for this meeting, but then not want to hear from people a week later."

Team building events don't create lasting change in isolation. The only way they catalyze sustainable change is to pair them with consistent, positive leadership behavior over time. No event is magical enough to create results if leaders aren't modeling the right behaviors.

Here's some advice I've given leaders during the planning stage on several occasions to help them get the most from the experience they're budgeting for:

Before the Event

- **Set the tone:** Discuss upcoming events with intentionality, keeping in mind that you influence how your team will approach them. Frame it as an opportunity to step away from the day-to-day and engage in valuable development, not as mandatory fun or another boring meeting.
- **Participate fully:** Engage authentically so you're giving your team permission to do the same. Don't check your email, text, or scroll during activities, make jokes that undermine the process, or judge team members for mistakes. This behavior works against success.

◆ **Share your purpose:** Help your team understand why you're excited about the event by discussing it as an investment in them, not just the company. You might also want to discuss the outcomes you're hoping for and why you chose the event based on your team's goals or company culture.

During the Event

◆ **Model vulnerability:** Let yourself be imperfect and make mistakes so you can learn alongside your team. This creates psychological safety for everyone. This behavior should continue after the event.
◆ **Support the process:** Trust your facilitator and the activities you selected. Don't jump in to explain or direct unless you're asked to. You want to participate at the same level as your team so they can relax around you.
◆ **Observe and learn:** Look for team dynamics that emerge, especially ones you don't usually see at the office. Notice who shines as a leader, problem-solver, or collaborator so you can go back and praise everyone based on their involvement and strengths.

After the Event

◆ **Follow through:** Regularly reflect on the insights gained during the event. Ask how people are applying what they learned or how it impacted them. This keeps momentum going, especially if you celebrate the wins your team had, even if you were "just playing games."
◆ **Reinforce changes:** Say something when you see your team applying new skills or communicating differently. Acknowledge, appreciate, and reward these moments. What gets recognized gets repeated. Celebrate mistakes too!
◆ **Plan continuity:** One event doesn't create lasting change. Plan follow-ups, check-ins, or additional development opportunities. Make team building a regular thing your staff can look forward to.

When leaders consistently follow through on these commitments, something remarkable happens. The lessons from a single event begin to reshape daily interactions and team culture.

The Art of Creating Moments That Transform

Remember, change happens in the time between activities, in the moments when people reflect on what just happened and begin to see each other differently. It's in the memory of a quiet team member leading their group to success, or when the team finally worked as a cohesive unit instead of a collection of brilliant individuals pulling in different directions.

The difference between boring team building and transformational events isn't found in the activities themselves. It's deeper.

The real shift happens when you create an intentional foundation based on an honest assessment of what the team truly needs. This kind of design helps people feel safe enough to try new things, make mistakes, and show up as themselves. From there, they can start to see the value in their differences, which naturally strengthens their ability to connect and collaborate.

Whether your team needs deeper connections, more creative breakthroughs, stronger collaboration, or something else entirely, you'll be more likely to get results when you follow the methods outlined in this chapter.

Team building has never been about forcing the beautifully diverse personalities and creative styles within a group to fit predetermined molds. It's about creating conditions where each person can shine and the group learns to work together in the most productive and fulfilling way possible.

It's no small thing when someone feels truly seen and appreciated by the people they work with. When an entire team experiences that, they begin to understand not only what they need to succeed, but also what their colleagues need to feel supported. They learn how to connect and communicate in ways that produce results everyone can be proud of.

This is how a team becomes something more than anyone thought possible. It's why some companies soar while others struggle to keep up. The best part? A transformation this powerful can begin with your next decision about your team, so make that choice intentional.

Now, with all of this in mind, get ready to get your hands dirty—we're digging into the actual games and activities next!

PART III

The Activities That Move Teams

In Parts I and II, we explored why team building works and how to approach it beforehand. Now it's time to look at what you'll actually be doing with your team—what these ideas look like in action.

These chapters include collections of icebreakers, games, and activities, with slightly less discussion, data, and theory. Think of Part III as your toolbox or vision board, and revisit it when you need something fresh for your crew.

Combining Innovation with Imitation

Before we jump into the activities, I want to share a moment that changed my approach to team building. I attended IMEX in 2014 and participated in a session led by a musical team building company.

During the presentation, the facilitator casually remarked that musicians are "the greatest thieves" because all songs use the same basic chords. Then, he asked the audience, "What's the difference between innovation and imitation?"

After some discussion, he said, "Innovation improves something through the changes made, while imitation is simply copying from someone else."

Harvard Business Review puts it similarly:

"Strictly defined, innovation occurs only when something is entirely new, having never been done before. When competitors in the same industry subsequently copy the innovator, even though it is something new for them, then it is not innovation; it is imitation."

This distinction reshaped how we design team building activities. When we add an iPad to a scavenger hunt, it's not innovation; it's just introducing tech to an existing idea. But when we redesigned TeamBonding's traditional Polaroid photo scavenger hunt to use an app for collaboration, GPS-based challenges, and instant sharing features that extend beyond the event—now *that's* innovation!

When I first started TeamBonding, one of my facilitators insisted we should only offer programs no one else had ever done. He believed clients only wanted originality. I saw things differently— clients wanted familiarity *and* novelty. They often booked something recognizable first, built trust in us, and then returned to try our innovative programs.

Finding a balance between innovation and imitation proved to be our key to growth and success. As Ohio State business professor Oded Shenkar put it in *Forbes*, the most successful companies "combine creativity and imitation" to build their own advantage. He calls them **imovators**—innovators who strategically apply imitation.

TeamBonding is an imovator, and I'm proud of that. I want you to become an imovator too—someone who knows when to innovate and when to iterate on what works.

From "Yes, and . . ." to Yes We Can!

Balancing innovation with familiarity is part of how we've designed these activities. We've also incorporated the famous improv principle of *"Yes, and . . ."* into almost everything we do. This technique taught me that the best experiences are often those we create to meet a specific need—when I say "Yes, and . . ." to my clients.

The activities in this part evolved from more than 35 years of this *"Yes, and . . ."* approach. Some we've refined over thousands of sessions, others we developed to address a unique challenge for a client.

All of them are grounded in the three-part framework I outlined at the start of Chapter 5: a clear foundation, a structured experience, and an intentional atmosphere.

What You'll Discover in Part III

♦ **Chapter 6: Energizers That Don't Make You Cringe**— Opening activities that we deem "energizers" designed to honor different personality types while building genuine connections. These aren't time-fillers; they're strategic relationship-building tools that set the tone for everything that follows.

♦ **Chapter 7: Games That Grow Teams**—Transformational experiences at the heart of great team building. Problem-solving, creativity exercises, communication activities, and improv-based sessions that build trust and adaptability.

♦ **Chapter 8: Giving Back Through Purpose-Driven Play**— CSR programs that create deeper bonds than traditional team building while making tangible impacts on communities. It's the ultimate triple win for teams, companies, and the people you serve.

♦ **Chapter 9: DIY TeamBonding**—High-impact experiences you can run anywhere, anytime, even without a big budget or dedicated facilitator. Most also include modifications that work for remote teams.

Meet Your Guides: Shannon Lane Dupont and Jayne Hannah

To bring you the most practical, field-tested insights for this section, I called on two of TeamBonding's most experienced professionals who've spent decades making team building work.

Shannon Lane DuPont has spent 17 years as a program developer at TeamBonding, creating the experiences behind many of our most successful experiences. She crafts activities that accomplish specific business outcomes and has run thousands of events for clients across nearly every industry.

Shannon has an uncanny ability to see why certain activities change teams while others don't, and she's a master of refining events through real-world implementation.

As Shannon puts it: "What I always hold onto is this: the thing that hits the most from an event is when you have some shared experience with the people around you. That really brings people together."

Jayne Hannah brings another valuable perspective with her 35 years of corporate planning experience. She's witnessed every type of team dynamic and organizational challenge firsthand. Jayne has used this experience to master the art of adapting on the fly, especially when things don't go according to plan (which happens a lot in team building). She's also our virtual events expert, having pioneered ways to make remote team building as impactful as in-person events.

Jayne's expertise was a huge part of why we continued to thrive when the pandemic forced everyone online, and so many people maintained invaluable connections thanks to her insights.

Jayne's philosophy is simple but powerful: "Everything we do is based on the pure ethics of working together—communication, support, listening. Even Outrageous Games are all about communicating and being an entire team supporting one another."

Together, Shannon and Jayne have spent thousands of hours designing, planning, and improving team building experiences for Fortune 500 companies, startups, nonprofits, and more. Their insights throughout these chapters come from real events, real teams, and real challenges.

In the pages ahead, we'll show you how to put what you've learned into practice—from quick, thoughtful openers that dissolve awkwardness, to powerful games that push growth, to service-driven programs that turn teamwork into impact. Each chapter builds on the last, guiding you from connection to collaboration to purpose.

CHAPTER 6

Energizers That Don't Make You Cringe

No one likes hearing the word "icebreaker" related to anything they're doing. It's like the collective eye-roll I mentioned earlier when someone kicks things off by talking about "team building and trust exercises." You can practically see dread ripple through the room as people shift in their seats, check their phones, close their eyes, or otherwise prepare themselves for 15 minutes of awkward, forced interaction.

They're waiting for it to end before it even begins, expecting something just as bad as every other icebreaker they've sat through.

"The minute that you say, say your name and where you're from and what's your favorite fruit, people just don't want to do that," says Jayne, laughing.

1. The problem isn't icebreakers themselves, but how often they're used to force participation, ignoring basic human psychology by putting people on the spot and expecting instant bonding. Especially when the activity has nothing to do with what's coming next. "Okay, everyone, we're here to do some team building today. We're going to do some icebreakers to get started!"

2. "Hey! We're getting ready for our scavenger hunt, but before we dive in, let's get the party started early with some energizers so we can all shake off the nerves, yeah?"

The delivery doesn't matter—no one responds well to the first example. But the second? That kind of opener can actually get people excited!

The Difference Between Cringe and Connection

Shannon Lane DuPont has been creating events for 17 years, and she's seen every possible variation of energizer success and failure. Her perspective on what works is similar to mine, and she got to the heart of it during our interview:

"I think that asking everyone to say something individually, like a get-to-know-you thing, is usually what people don't like. The icebreakers people enjoy are the ones that engage everyone simultaneously in the same experience. They unite people instead of singling them out."

When you make people go around the room sharing their names, where they're from, and their favorite fruits—or worse, their biggest regrets—you're basically putting them on stage for solo performances while everyone else judges. Even if that judgment is positive, the experience still feels exposed and artificial. I cringed just writing the "biggest regret" part. I've been in the room when someone used that as an icebreaker (after introducing it as such), and I saw the ripple of dread.

Compare that to activities where everyone is moving, participating, and discovering things together. Suddenly, people aren't worried about how they sound or whether their answer is clever enough. They're just engaged in a shared experience.

"I also think it's really important to have an energizer that combines physicality with energy and then a little bit of whatever the activity is," Shannon adds. "I like to get them out of their chairs to form a circle and create a new group."

Physical movement literally breaks people out of their default positions and mindsets. Sitting in the same chair you always sit in, next to the same people you always sit next to, keeps your brain in familiar patterns. But standing up and moving into a new configuration primes your brain for new interactions and possibilities.

Example Energizer: Commonalities

One of Shannon's favorite energizers demonstrates these principles. It's called Commonalities, and it's deceptively simple. She starts by asking everyone to stand up and form groups based on the type of toothpaste they use. Groups form with everybody who uses Crest, Colgate, prescription toothpaste, and so on.

Then they move through new rounds with different categories, each of which adds constraints to make it more engaging. By the end, if it fits your group's comfort level, you might have something like, "Now group up by your favorite animal, but you're not allowed to tell each other what it is! You have to make whatever noise that animal makes or draw the animal on a sticky note."

Adding the option to draw the animal on a sticky note opens up the fun to people with different comfort levels. Jayne, for example, says, "Anything to do with mimicking an animal makes me cringe. I don't like it, but I still love Commonalities! It's tons of fun to find someone who's born in the same month as you, and it's great when you make it faster and more challenging."

Regardless of what everyone picks, you'll suddenly have professionals meowing like cats or drawing dogs and showing everyone, and it works because it's ridiculous. People are laughing, they're being silly together, and they're learning about their colleagues.

"Things like this feel safer when you're doing them with a group instead of being put in the spotlight," Shannon adds. "If it's silly, everyone is silly together, creating a moment of shared vulnerability that traditional introductions simply can't match."

Now, let's take a quick look at why this event is so effective.

The Power of Simultaneous Engagement

Commonalities uses simultaneous engagement for a reason—it taps into core elements of human psychology. When a group does the same thing at the same time, several powerful effects occur:

- ◆ **Diffusion of attention:** No one person is the center of focus, which helps people feel more comfortable and present.
- ◆ **Shared vulnerability:** Everyone's in it together. This creates safe, collective vulnerability that forges strong bonds.

- **Social proof:** Watching others participate and mess up makes it feel normal and safe. People don't just hear "it's okay to fail"—they see it.
- **Collective energy:** Group momentum and shared enthusiasm have a powerful psychological effect. Even research shows group workouts are more beneficial than solo ones.[1]

Moving and making animal noises together is way more comfortable than doing it solo because group action reduces the feeling of exposure.

Movement Changes Mindset

Another big reason Commonalities works is that it gets people to stand up and walk around. Physical activity changes brain chemistry and group dynamics. When people move, several things happen:

- **Blood flow to the brain increases**, improving cognition
- **Endorphins are released**, boosting mood
- **Spatial memories form**, making the experience more memorable
- **Social barriers drop** through casual proximity

Some of these, like improved mood, are well-known benefits of exercise. Others, like reduced social barriers, happen simply because the group is doing something together instead of sitting still.

The Psychology of Good Energizers

Psychological safety is the foundation of all meaningful engagement, and it's the secret to good energizers. As we discussed at length in Part I, people are more likely to connect authentically when they feel safe.

Effective energizers foster psychological safety while cringeworthy ones violate it.

What to look for in effective energizers:

- Everyone engages together
- Everyone is silly at the same time (if it's silly)

- People can choose their level of sharing and comfort
- The goal is curiosity, laughter, and conversation, not performance

What to watch out for in ineffective (or damaging) icebreakers:

- People are put on the spot, causing anxiety
- People risk looking silly or facing embarrassment alone
- The activity forces openness and personal disclosure

Another big part of what helps an energizer land is whether or not it's a good fit for the team.

Adapting to Team Dynamics
Even if you're using effective energizers instead of ineffective icebreakers, each team will respond differently. Use your best judgment and try to pick ones that match the group's vibe. Here are some examples:

For Analytical Teams

- **Use logic-based activities** like categorization or pattern-finding
- **Provide clear rules** and measurable outcomes (points, completion times, specific goals)
- **Avoid vague prompts**—connect activities to work applications

Example: "We're going to see how quickly you can organize yourselves by birthday month. Then we'll discuss the communication strategies that emerged."

For Creative Teams

- **Embrace open-ended exploration** and multiple "right" answers
- **Include visual or artistic elements** when possible
- **Celebrate unexpected outcomes** and creative interpretations

Example: Use the "Yes, and . . ." principle from improv to practice building on ideas rather than shooting them down.

For Introverted Teams

- **Provide thinking time** before requiring participation
- **Use written elements** (chat, notes, individual reflection), and avoid putting people in the spotlight
- **Create smaller group interactions** before large group sharing

Example: Give people two minutes to write down their "Two Truths and a Lie" before anyone shares verbally.

For Extroverted Teams

- **Use high-energy, verbal activities** that let people shine provide chances for different people to lead
- **Include competitive elements** and public recognition
- **Allow for spontaneous conversation** and tangents

Example: Fast-paced games like "Coffee Pot" where people can jump in with guesses and questions.

For New Teams

- **Focus on discovery** and learning basic information with structured sharing that feels comfortable
- **Include visual elements** that make people memorable
- **Create multiple touchpoints** for connection throughout the event

Example: Try energizers like "Like it. Pin it. Own it." to help people learn about their colleagues at their own pace.

For Established Teams

- **Go deeper** than basic getting-to-know-you information; focus on new perspectives
- **Challenge assumptions** people might have about each other
- **Include work-related reflection** and process improvement

Example: Try activities like "Office Bingo" to reward people who take time to get to know their teammates.

Now that you understand what makes energizers work and how to match them to your team, here are nine proven options you can use immediately.

9 Fast, Fun, and Surprisingly Effective Energizers

Well-designed, simple energizers like Commonalities can transform an entire room. This section includes several of our favorite activities, and they all work for the same simple reason: they make connections feel easy.

Whether it's pins, colors, or quick games, the goal isn't the activity, but the chemistry it creates. You'll notice they all share common traits that make them fun instead of forced, safe instead of stressful, and surprisingly effective at building real bonds.

Don't be fooled by the short, simple descriptions—each of these yields great results!

Energizer #1. Like It. Pin It. Own It

This one's good for helping people connect every day by sparking natural conversation between peers and encouraging people to find common ground. It uses lapel pins, but you can make it virtual by using status messages instead.

What You Need

- ◆ Blank lapel pins (enough for everyone)
- ◆ Sharpies or magic markers
- ◆ A basket

How It Works

1. Team members work together writing statements that people can identify with on pins. For example:
   a. "I'm an animal lover!"
   b. "I've read all 8 Harry Potter books."
   c. "I speak multiple languages."

2. Place all the pins in a basket by the front door.

3. Ask people to choose a pin from the basket they can relate to and wear it for the day.

4. Ask everyone to return the pins to the basket when they leave and pick a new one the next day. Try keeping an extensive collection of pins and refreshing the statements every few weeks to keep it interesting. You can also try themed weeks and question pins.

Jayne's Virtual Event Reminder

It might surprise you that people are willing to be just as competitive and playful on a screen as they are in person! Perhaps for some of them, they're even more willing because they're in their safe space, at home, so they feel like they can be a little bit more playful without going wrong in front of anyone or falling flat on their face.

Just remember, energy is all about the planning. Make sure you have enough people and facilitators, test everything, pick good music, and welcome them with enthusiasm.

Energizer #2: Agree or Disagree

This one's a great option for sparking friendly debate among teams that enjoy a bit of intellectual sparring. It's a simple whiteboard game that can help team members understand different perspectives, and it works just as well in group chat channels.

What You Need

- ◆ Large whiteboard hung in a common area
- ◆ Whiteboard markers

How It Works

1. At the start of the week, ask one team member to write a statement on a whiteboard above "Agree" and "Disagree" columns. It's best to avoid political and deeply personal topics, instead opting for more lighthearted statements like:
   a. "The Patriots are the best NFL team."
   b. "Pineapple belongs on pizza."
   c. "Morning people are more successful than night owls."
2. Ask people to sign their names under "Agree" or "Disagree" as they pass by throughout the week.

Energizer #3: Office Bingo

This one combines bingo with discovering unknown facts about teammates, helping everyone get to know their peers better. You can generate custom bingo cards online if you're running it virtually.

What You Need

◆ Custom bingo cards with team member names
◆ Unknown facts collected from each person
◆ Bingo markers or pens
◆ Small prizes (optional)

How It Works

1. Collect one unknown fact from each team member ahead of time. Here are some examples:
   a. "This person has never eaten sushi."
   b. "This person once met a celebrity on a plane."
   c. "This person speaks four languages."
2. Create bingo cards with names arranged randomly.
3. Pass out the cards and read numbered facts to start the game. For example, "Number 15: This person hates dairy products, especially yogurt."

4. If people know who it is, they mark that name. Ask everyone to put their markers down, confirm the name, and repeat.

5. First person to complete a row (or full card) wins.

Energizer #4: Coffee Pot

This one is fun for lunch breaks, video calls, or any time your crew needs a quick mental energizer and some good laughs.

What You Need

- ◆ Your team

How It Works

1. One person thinks of a verb and writes it down privately.
2. Everyone guesses the verb by asking questions.
3. The person answering can only use "coffee pot" (or your company name) instead of the actual verb.
4. Continue until someone guesses the verb correctly.

Here's an example of how this might play out:

- ◆ "How do you get to work each day?"
- ◆ "I coffee pot to the subway station, then take the train."
- ◆ "What do you do for exercise?"
- ◆ "I go to the gym, but I also coffee pot when the weather is nice."
- ◆ "Do you coffee pot fast or slow?"
- ◆ "Pretty fast—I'm trying to improve my time."
- ◆ "Are you running?"
- ◆ "YES!"

Energizer #5: Lifestyle Show and Tell

This is a remote-first game. It uses a "Lifestyles of the Rich and Famous" approach to let people showcase their personality and work environment in authentic, personal ways.

What You Need

◆ Your team

How It Works

1. Ask each person to give a 2–3 minute tour of their home office or something meaningful from their environment. For example:
   a. "Here's my incredibly organized desk setup."
   b. "Here's the five-kilometer race medal that keeps me motivated."
   c. "Meet my office assistant!" (introduces their pet)

Energizer #6: Virtual Four Corners

This one works great for helping everyone learn each other's preferences and get insights into their colleagues. It works just as well virtually as it does in person.

What You Need

◆ Four colored items like markers, clothing, and books for each person (in-person, you just need one set of four items)

How It Works

1. For video calls, each person keeps all four objects on their desk. If you're in person, put one object in each corner of the room.
2. Present multiple-choice questions to help people learn each other's preferences, then have them hold up or stand near their selected color. I keep it lighthearted with questions like:
   a. "If you could own any vehicle, what would it be? Orange for Tesla, green for Harley Davidson, red for Sports Car, blue for truck."
   b. "Where would you go for your ideal vacation? Orange for beach, green for mountains, red for city, blue for countryside."

Energizer #7: Color Challenge

This is a quick activity designed to boost energy and morale. It works in person, but I prefer it virtually.

What You Need

- ◆ Your team

How It Works

1. Pick a color and give everyone two minutes to leave and collect as much of it as possible. Tell them that points are awarded for creativity, quantity, or the most ridiculous implementation.
2. Ask people to come back *wearing* the color if you think your team would be up for it.
3. When everyone returns, award points for standout efforts. For extra energy, offer small prizes like candy bars or gift cards.

Energizer #8: Mighty Minis

Use this one to tap into your team's creativity or break out of a funk. It's an observation and guessing game that works well virtually or in person.

What You Need

- ◆ Office supplies or household objects
- ◆ Smartphones (or webcams if remote)

How It Works

1. Ask everyone to find an object that looks mysterious up close.
2. If you're in person, ask them they take a close-up photo and return. If you're virtual, have them hold it to their webcam or send a photo in chat.

3. Go around the group and have everyone guess what each object is. Here are some examples of tricky close-ups:
   a. Stapler
   b. Zipper
   c. Sponge
   d. Shoe tread
4. Award points for correct guesses and let participants take turns as the "holder," and always allow time for funny wrong guesses.

Energizer #9: Two Truths and a Lie

This is a classic that works in almost any meeting format and lightens the mood. It's great for helping everyone learn a bit about their peers in a snap.

What You Need

◆ Your team

How It Works

1. Give participants a few minutes to prepare three statements—two true, one false. Encourage them to make the truths sound unbelievable and the lies sound plausible, while staying within their comfort zone. For example:
   a. "I've done CPR successfully on someone."
   b. "I've met two Canadian prime ministers."
   c. "I've traveled to seven different countries."
2. Let the group vote on the lie, then have the person reveal the answer. They can share more details if they want, but never pressure them.

Planning and Executing Great Energizers

Beyond choosing the right activity, the following are execution principles that separate good energizers from great ones:

Planning Tip #1: Keep Directions Minimal

Ever listened to someone read all the instructions for a board game in one go? For most of us, it's a near-instant brain melt. Many people can't process long instructions without losing interest.

Keep directions short, know the activity well, prep a concise version of the rules as talking points, and get to the fun quickly. That's why many TeamBonding activities are based on familiar games like Trivial Pursuit, Jeopardy, or 20 Questions—it removes the need for long explanations.

Planning Tip #2: Make Everything Inclusive

Group activities should be inclusive so everyone feels respected and seen. Every team includes people from different backgrounds, cultures, generations, and identities. Make sure your activities and questions respect everyone, no matter their life experience.

This is especially important for remote teams, where people may be spread across the country or around the world. It's important to consider:

◆ Time zones
◆ Energy levels
◆ Cultural differences
◆ Comfort with sharing
◆ Language barriers
◆ Communication styles
◆ Different living situations
◆ Privacy needs
◆ Personality types (introverts versus extroverts)

Take time to get to know your team members so you have enough personal knowledge of everyone to take the appropriate precautions.

Execution Tip #1: Stop When It's Most Fun (Seriously)

It's a common instinct to try to keep activities going as long as possible when the group is having fun, but it can lead to boredom. It might feel counterintuitive, but ending on a high note leaves people with a positive memory and makes them want to do it again.

You'll know you've hit peak engagement when you see the most laughter, hear people talking over each other with excitement, or notice even the quietest person is fully participating.

So, watch for peak engagement and, when you find it, start looking for your moment to end the activity. Make sure everyone has had a chance to participate, of course, but wrap things up once you know you're not cutting anyone off.

Execution Tip #2: Switch Up the Energy Often

It's easy for people's brains to shut down when they're doing the same thing for too long. Switching up the energy when it drags is a great way to keep everyone engaged.

I like to alternate between things like this during meetings, group activities, or team events:

- Sitting and standing activities
- Individual and group participation
- Verbal and visual engagement
- High energy and reflective moments

Don't just tell everyone to stand and then keep monologuing—actually switch things up. Think about times you've needed to stay awake. What do you do when you start to nod off? You change your stimuli to wake up your brain!

Common Icebreaker Mistakes and How to Avoid Them

After watching thousands of icebreakers succeed and fail, here are the most common pitfalls and how to avoid them:

Mistake #1: The Endless Round-Robin

What it looks like: "Let's go around the room and everyone share your name, role, and one interesting fact about yourself."

Why it fails: By the seventh person, everyone's mentally checked out. People are either dreading their turn or thinking about what they'll say instead of listening.

Better approach: Try simultaneous sharing activities where everyone participates at once, like grouping by commonalities or holding up colored items.

Mistake #2: The Overshare Invitation

What it looks like: "Tell us about a challenge you've overcome" or "Share something personal that shaped who you are."

Why it fails: You're asking for vulnerability before trust is established. People either share too much (making others uncomfortable) or share too little (feeling like they failed).

Better approach: Start with preferences and opinions, build to personal experiences once people feel safe.

Mistake #3: The Rushed Introduction

What it looks like: "We have a lot to cover today, so let's do a quick icebreaker."

Why it fails: If you don't have time to do it well, don't do it at all. Rushing makes it feel like a checkbox activity rather than a genuine opportunity for connection.

Better approach: Either allocate sufficient time for meaningful interaction or skip the energizer and dive into your content.

Mistake #4: The Activity Without Purpose

What it looks like: Using icebreakers that have no connection to your meeting purpose or team goals.

Why it fails: People sense when activities feel disconnected from the real work, making them feel like time-wasters.

Better approach: Choose activities that connect thematically to your meeting purpose or that practice skills you'll need in your session.

Ready, Set, Connect

The energizers in this chapter are designed to help people feel safe enough to become curious about their colleagues and get to know each other on a deeper level. If you use them often, you can completely change how your team interacts.

But energizers are just the appetizer! They get people comfortable and engaged so they're ready to go deeper!

Next, we'll move beyond these quick activities and into complete team building experiences that can create huge breakthrough moments. These are the events people remember years later because they transform groups into genuine teams. Let's get into it.

CHAPTER 7

Games That Grow Teams

When adults play the right games together, they develop trust and connection in real time. Some of the best feedback we've received has been about events like these.

One of my favorites was a call from a client three months after we ran a *Beat the Box* event. "David, I have to ask . . . what sort of black magic did you work? My team's completely different! They're listening to each other and solving problems without coming to me about every single issue. I hardly know how to react. Whatever you did stuck. I want to schedule another event now because I'm never going back to how things were before."

We didn't do anything mysterious. We just helped them play the right game for their needs and let them work it out together.

The first 10 minutes with her team were chaos—twenty brilliant, analytical accountants talking over each other, trying to solve everything individually. Around the 12-minute mark, something shifted. Someone said, "Okay, everyone, stop. What if we organized this differently? We're not going to win at this rate." Everyone listened up at that last line.

That's where the shift happened. They started working together, coordinating, listening, and actually functioning as a team. By the time the clock counted down, they'd completed all the challenges and were high-fiving. They'd discovered something that changed how they approached problems.

The Framework for Growth-Oriented Team Activities

Over the years, we've found specific elements that separate shared activities from transformational experiences and distilled them into this basic framework we use as a checklist when developing growth-oriented team activities:

Meaningful Challenge

The activity must present a real challenge that pushes team members past their comfort zones. These challenges get people to pay attention, think creatively, develop new approaches, and rely on teammates.

It's about finding the sweet spot where challenge level matches skill level. When you find that balance, people engage, grow, and change how they interact and approach things.

Interdependence

Growth-oriented games must demand genuine collaboration. Success depends on all members working together, and failure if they don't. This might mean:

◆ Information that's distributed across team members
◆ Tasks that require multiple skill sets
◆ Complex challenges or too many moving parts for any individual to solve alone
◆ Time constraints that necessitate teamwork

Real Consequences

The brain responds to consequences—most of us want to avoid them. You need genuine outcomes that matter, even if the stakes are playful. Generally, consequences revolve around not winning a desirable prize, whether bragging rights, time off, a gift card, or something else.

The right incentive depends on the people and team, but here are some examples of how to set up activities with real consequences:

◆ Competition with other teams
◆ Time pressure that creates urgency
◆ Quality standards that require excellence
◆ Public presentation of results

Post-Event Reflection

The role of reflection in learning and growth cannot be understated. It's proven to increase learning and engagement and is seeing increased use in professional and educational settings.[1] I always suggest scheduling post-event reflection, both formally and informally. When possible, I weave reflection into the games themselves, creating opportunities to:

- Analyze what happened and why
- Identify successful strategies and approaches
- Recognize breakdown points and missed opportunities
- Connect lessons to real work situations
- Commit to applying insights going forward

"The shared experience you have with the people around you is what matters, whether it's a shared purpose—you're all working towards collecting donations for something—or a shared unique experience," says Shannon. "That really brings people together. The fun and games are important, but the end goal is that they're forcing you to connect in a unique way, do something outside your comfort zone, and learn something new about the person you're working with."

Games for Problem-Solving and Collaboration

Teams that can solve problems together under pressure have a competitive advantage in any business environment. It's common to see disjointed teams that refuse to or don't know how to collaborate. They try to solve problems individually and step on each other's toes.

Likewise, teams that know how to collaborate can fail to solve even basic problems if they lack experience or confidence in the necessary skills. That's why I've developed games targeting this set of issues.

The key is creating scenarios that mirror workplace challenges while keeping the stakes playful enough to encourage experimentation and risk-taking.

The games in this section aren't just my go-tos—they're top picks from Shannon, Jayne, and other facilitators. These experiences regularly create breakthrough moments like the one at the beginning of this chapter. They help teams see what's possible when they tackle problems together, and I'm proud of the feedback they bring in.

Beat the Box

This is one of TeamBonding's signature problem-solving experiences, and it's Shannon's favorite. "I love watching teams transform right in front of my eyes with this one," she says. "They move from confusion to full cooperation, and it's reaffirming for everything we do to see people have those *aha* moments. I also love hearing leaders gush about the difference this game makes back at the office!"

The Challenge

Teams race against the clock to unlock a series of four interconnected boxes, each containing increasingly complex escape room-style challenges. There are no lengthy introductions—just a short, thrilling video that catapults players into the game. Each challenge must be solved in sequence, with complexity increasing at each stage.

The ultimate goal: discover the mystery slogan that can stop the clock before time runs out.

The Journey

Initially, chaos reigns. Team members grab different puzzles, everyone has opinions about the right approach, and people try to solve everything individually. As time pressure builds and complexity increases, the team realizes they need each other to succeed.

The Transformation

Once this realization hits, the gamification design kicks in and engagement intensifies. People naturally start organizing within their teams. Someone becomes the timekeeper, tracking minutes. Another manages solved clues and catalogs what's been discovered. A coordinator emerges to direct efforts between sub-teams working on different puzzles.

Communication becomes clearer and more purposeful. Efforts synchronize. The team functions as a unit, combining individual skillsets to achieve what they couldn't accomplish alone.

Key Learning Elements

- **Communication Under Pressure:** Teams learn to share information quickly and clearly when stakes feel real.
- **Resource Management:** Limited tools force teams to prioritize and tap into strategic thinking.
- **Role Emergence:** People discover unexpected strengths, and natural leaders surface.
- **Distributed Leadership:** Success requires multiple people stepping up at different moments.

The Infinite Loop

This represents the next evolution in team problem-solving experiences. While virtual reality is more common in entertainment and training, this activity holds a special place in TeamBonding's history as the first VR-powered team challenge.

The Challenge

Teams are split into two groups with different realities. Half don VR headsets to become characters on a mission to save a man trapped in the digital realm. The other half remains in the physical room with no view into the virtual environment.

No one has the complete picture, so success depends on how precisely and effectively the two groups communicate across divided realities.

The more effectively VR players describe what they're facing, the faster their real-world teammates can find the solution. Only one team can solve the challenge first.

The Journey

The VR group encounters puzzles and obstacles in the virtual world they must describe to their physical-world teammates. The physical team has resources, information, or tools the VR group needs but can't access.

The initial moments are disorienting. The VR team tries to describe what they're seeing, but their words feel inadequate. It can sound like this:

"There's a blue thing!"
"Which blue thing?"
"The one by the . . . the structure!"
"What structure? I don't see a structure!"

Much like how new teams operate before finding their rhythm, early communication is clumsy, filled with miscommunication or assumptions, and frustration builds quickly. This continues until everyone sees it happening and realizes they'll need to solve the communication breakdown to win the game.

The Transformation

Once the VR and physical-world teams realize the communication breakdown, they begin creating protocols, considering the other team's experiences, and slowing down for clarity. That earlier mess of cross-talk evolves into exchanges like:

"There's a cylindrical blue object, about waist-height, with three red symbols on top."
"Okay, is there anything around it?"
"Yes, it's beside a building-height rectangular tower, but it doesn't seem important—it lacks defining features."

Natural roles emerge: some excel at describing, others at interpreting or coordinating. Players develop empathy—the VR team appreciates how hard it is to assist them when their counterparts can see what they're seeing, while the physical team learns how challenging it is for their VR counterparts to explain complex topics under pressure and starts asking clarifying questions before jumping into solutions.

Each failed attempt teaches something new about communicating better, and trust deepens as everyone overcomes the problem together.

Key Learning Elements

- **Communication Precision:** Teams discover how much clarity matters when context isn't shared and reinforce that vague descriptions lead nowhere.
- **Role Flexibility:** People naturally gravitate toward roles that match their strengths in describing, interpreting, or coordinating.
- **Trust Under Uncertainty:** The VR group must act on information from teammates operating with incomplete knowledge.
- **Continuous Feedback:** The iterative nature emphasizes that improvement comes from learning from each attempt.
- **Perspective Taking:** Each group develops genuine empathy for the unique challenges their teammates face.

Build-a-Boat

This is a hands-on challenge combining creative problem-solving with real-world feedback and literal sink-or-swim consequences.

The Challenge

Teams split into groups, each using basic materials to construct a floating vessel capable of carrying them across a body of water. To earn more tools and materials, they compete in fast-paced mini-games testing skills like quick thinking and coordination.

Once finished, boats face two tests. First, teams impress a panel of judges with a sales pitch highlighting innovation and design flair. Then comes the moment of truth as teams race across the water, either paddling to victory or providing entertainment as their boats sink.

The Journey

The planning phase reveals how teams approach uncertainty. Some dive into construction, only to realize halfway through they needed a plan. Others debate designs endlessly, watching time tick away. Teams must balance creative ambition with engineering reality. That design might look cool, but will it float?

As construction begins, resource management becomes critical. Limited materials force trade-off decisions. Should we reinforce the hull or build better propulsion? Different members contribute different skills—some gravitate toward design, others to construction, others to testing and iteration.

Earned-resource challenges add pressure, forcing teams to coordinate who tackles which mini-game while others keep building.

The Transformation

Few challenges provide immediate, undeniable feedback like this one. When boats sink or float, abstract evaluation disappears, and teams experience the full design cycle—execution, assessment, and iteration—in three hours or less. The combination of creativity and engineering reveals diverse capabilities while requiring genuine collaboration.

As Shannon puts it: "Some boats sink spectacularly. Some sail across the water. Either way, teams discover how planning, resource-sharing, and quick pivots make all the difference. The lessons tend to stick, too, because this isn't something you forget even if you don't take a dip!"

Key Learning Elements

- ◆ **Creative Problem-Solving:** Teams balance innovation with practical engineering constraints while strengthening resource management skills. Time pressure requires quick prototyping, testing, and improvement.
- ◆ **Role Coordination:** Different skills emerge naturally and teams must decide on roles like designers, builders, testers, and strategists.
- ◆ **Immediate Feedback:** Unlike many workplace projects, success or failure is unmistakably clear and instant.
- ◆ **Cross-Team Learning:** Watching different approaches and outcomes provides valuable comparative insights.

Product Pipeline

Jayne uses this activity to demonstrate emotional intelligence in action, calling it one of the most effective ways to reveal how people respond under complex, shifting pressures.

"Emotional intelligence is your awareness of how you react in certain situations," explains Jayne. "It's about recognizing when you're feeling overwhelmed—that fight-or-flight response—and learning to hold tight, calm down, and see what your opportunities are in that moment."

This event also serves as a physical metaphor of delivering a product to customers, which mirrors real organizational dynamics.

The Challenge

Teams represent departments, each working within an 8-foot square to build their section of a pipeline that must carry marbles (products) from start to finish and meet a minimum revenue requirement. Each department has a limited budget for materials like tape and twine. Two project managers oversee the big picture and uncover customer needs, while a marketing team crafts a pitch for the final product.

The catch? Sections must connect seamlessly with neighboring teams while working around complications, including changing instructions, strict quality standards, space restrictions, and mounting time pressure. Sections must operate harmoniously, and teams must balance their own function with cross-team collaboration.

The Journey

At first, teams focus on their own section. Project managers try to communicate the big picture, but most are too absorbed in immediate problems to listen. Budgets force tough choices. Marketing works in isolation, disconnected from what other teams are building.

As time pressure mounts, space constraints make coordination harder. Instructions shift. Some team members stay calm, others struggle. The emotional dynamic becomes as complex as the task itself.

The Transformation

Eventually, teams realize their section is meaningless if it doesn't connect. Project managers' roles become clear. Teams begin sharing information and helping neighbors. Quiet individuals start supporting stressed teammates.

The big moment arrives when the first marble enters the pipeline. Will it travel smoothly, or hit an obstacle? Success or not, teams immediately see how their actions shaped the result. The physical pipeline becomes an undeniable representation of how well they collaborated across boundaries.

Here's a question Jayne likes to ask teams: "With the time limits, with the space restrictions, with the constantly changing instructions—how did you feel personally, and how do you feel that created something positive or negative in your team?"

Key Learning Elements

- **Self-Awareness:** Participants discover their personal reactions to pressure and change.
- **Adaptability:** Working with shifting requirements forces teams to get comfortable with rapid pivoting.
- **Cross-Functional Collaboration:** Department structure mirrors real organizational dynamics and teaches communication between teams.
- **Relationship Management:** People learn how important it is to support struggling colleagues under pressure.

Remote Problem-Solving Games

The shift to remote and hybrid work has increased the need for effective ways to improve problem-solving and collaboration. If you've ever been part of the WFH crew, you're likely familiar with the issues that remote teams face.

When working with people you don't see regularly, or colleagues you've never met, communication must be explicit because you don't get nonverbal cues. Coordination requires different strategies and more careful approaches, but that also makes remote problem-solving valuable training.

These virtual problem-solving games force people to use the precision and care that remote work demands. When you can't point or rely on body language, you must communicate with a level of specificity that often exceeds what's needed in person. Teams that master virtual problem-solving bring those skills back to remote work and into the office if they're on a hybrid schedule.

The best remote problem-solving experiences require true collaboration, time-pressured decision-making, and equal participation regardless of personality. They also tend to offer immediate feedback and create safe spaces for technical mistakes, reflecting real challenges of remote work.

Jayne's Virtual Event Reminder

Strong, important connections can still be made when you're remote. It doesn't matter if you've got 600 people in an event or 20. The important part is the planning. For instance, if you have a huge group, make sure you're using breakout rooms! It makes those connections easier for everyone.

AI Takeover Challenge

This hacker-themed virtual experience immerses teams in a retro world of tech espionage where they must reboot collaboration skills to outmaneuver a rogue bot. We designed this with distributed teams in mind, crafting a smartphone-based game that tests communication, coordination, and collaboration through challenges that mirror the complexity of remote work.

The Challenge

Teams face a rogue bot that's taken control of critical systems. They tackle retro-style challenges—puzzles, word games, and cryptic clues—each designed to block progress and test their ability to think quickly under pressure.

Success requires decoding the bot's defenses, unraveling mysteries, and executing a digital heist that demands seamless teamwork. The experience ends with a reveal and video review showcasing team performance and identifying opportunities to strengthen collaboration.

The Journey

Initially, team members approach challenges individually, trying to solve puzzles on their own devices. The retro styling and cryptic clues create confusion. People talk over each other in video calls, share information haphazardly, and struggle to coordinate who's working on what. The bot seems to be winning as minutes tick away and challenges remain unsolved.

The virtual format amplifies remote work frustrations. People can't see what others are looking at, screen sharing becomes clunky, and the smartphone-based format means everyone's looking at different things. Some team members forge ahead while others fall behind, creating coordination gaps.

The Transformation

Then teams hit a challenge complex enough that individual effort clearly won't work. Someone suggests a system: "Let's have one person read the clue out loud while someone else takes notes." Roles emerge naturally: a coordinator who keeps track of solved and unsolved elements, a communicator who ensures everyone understands the current challenge, and specialists who excel at particular puzzle types.

The virtual environment that seemed like a hindrance becomes an advantage. Teams learn to use screen sharing strategically, develop protocols for who speaks when, and discover that written chat can clarify what verbal communication misses. Quick thinking accelerates as teams learn to delegate rapidly and trust each other's contributions without needing to oversee every detail. By the final challenges, what once felt chaotic now flows smoothly, like a well-oiled collaboration machine.

Key Learning Elements

- **Digital Coordination:** Teams develop systems to efficiently share information across screens and devices.
- **Equal Contribution:** Physical presence advantages disappear, and success depends purely on contribution quality.
- **Quick Decision-Making:** Time pressure forces teams to delegate, trust, and move forward without perfect information.
- **Role Flexibility:** People discover strengths in pattern recognition, coordination, or maintaining calm under pressure.
- **Asynchronous Collaboration:** Some challenges can be worked out independently before they're synthesized, which mirrors real remote work patterns.

Virtual Escape Rooms

What started as physical rooms with locks, keys, and hidden clues has evolved into digital experiences adapted to remote team development. These app- and web-based activities bring the escape room challenge to distributed teams, creating scenarios where collaboration isn't optional—it's the only path to success.

The Challenge

Teams face themed scenarios ranging from mobster chases to haunted houses to holiday heists. Regardless of theme, the core challenge remains: participants hunt for clues, solve brain teasers, crack codes, and pool resources to escape before time runs out.

These experiences leverage what virtual environments can do that physical spaces can't, including interactive scenes teams navigate together, puzzle elements requiring multiple people to contribute, and challenges designed to mirror workplace coordination needs.

The Journey

Teams break into smaller groups, typically guided by a facilitator who ensures the experience runs smoothly. The first puzzles seem straightforward, but complexity escalates. Some team members are naturally drawn to certain challenge types—word puzzles, visual patterns, logical deduction—while others feel stuck. The clock creates pressure.

Digital interfaces introduce frustrations. Someone's screen won't load. Another can't hear properly. A third found a clue but can't figure out how to share it. These technical challenges mirror the friction of remote work, where technology can be both enabler and obstacle.

The Transformation

Teams develop precise, clear communication while working with a remote/physical split, and that's a skill that transfers directly to remote work. The remote/physical split forces perspective-taking and builds empathy for colleagues with different information. This allows natural roles to emerge, revealing hidden leadership and coordination capabilities.

This also highlights unexpected advantages, like how quieter team members often contribute more in virtual environments where they can type observations without interrupting.

Key Learning Elements

- ◆ **Communication Protocol Development:** Successful teams create systems for efficiently sharing information across virtual space.
- ◆ **Role Recognition:** Teams discover strengths—pattern recognition, coordination, creative thinking, staying calm under pressure.
- ◆ **Patience Through Technical Challenges:** Digital interfaces teach teams to support each other through technological friction.
- ◆ **Creative Problem-Solving:** Virtual environments enable puzzles impossible in physical spaces, rewarding innovation.
- ◆ **Time Management:** The clock forces prioritization—what to tackle first, when to move on from dead ends.
- ◆ **Inclusive Participation:** Virtual formats often equalize participation, allowing personality types to contribute in ways that suit them.

The Science of Problem-Solving Under Pressure
The effectiveness of problem-solving activities comes from the rare combination of psychological safety and engaging challenges. It's a pair that triggers real, lasting learning.

Most workplaces offer one or the other—safe spaces with low stakes or high-pressure settings with consequences. Problem-solving games hit the sweet spot between them. Challenges are real enough to capture full attention, with stakes playful enough that failure becomes a teacher, not a threat.

When Failure Becomes Your Competitive Advantage
One thing that separates thriving companies from struggling ones is the acceptance of mistakes—intentional, accepted failure is part of their DNA, putting them leagues ahead of the competition.

These organizations understand something fundamental: innovation requires experimentation, and experimentation produces failure. The question isn't whether your team will fail, it's whether they'll feel safe enough to experiment and learn from the ones that don't work.

Problem-solving activities foster this safety. When the stakes are a puzzle box that won't open, a pipeline that leaks marbles, or a cardboard boat that might sink, people experiment freely. That freedom builds the confidence to try new approaches, the resilience to bounce back, and the innovative thinking companies need when real challenges arise.

I've watched this transformation hundreds of times: a team struggles, tries three failed approaches, finally succeeds on the fourth, and walks away changed. Remember that accounting team from the beginning of this chapter? That's exactly what they experienced.

That's the lesson they carry back to their desks, project meetings, or difficult client situations.

The Failure-Learning Cycle in Action

This is all about the psychological process teams experience through failure:

Experimentation

When consequences feel playful rather than professional, people try approaches they'd never risk at work. The cautious analyst suggests a wild idea. The reserved engineer takes charge. The by-the-book manager advocates breaking the rules. Teams discover capabilities in themselves and each other that standard environments keep hidden.

Immediate Feedback

Results arrive quickly and undeniably. The approach works or it doesn't. The boat sinks or floats. The puzzle unlocks or stays sealed. This immediacy is crucial. In most projects, teams wait weeks or months to see if their approach succeeded. That delay makes learning difficult. Problem-solving games compress feedback to minutes, allowing rapid testing, learning, and adaptation.

Adaptation
With clear feedback, teams pivot. They don't just try the same approach harder—they rethink strategy. Someone asks, "What if we're solving the wrong problem?" Another says, "Maybe we need to reorganize our roles." The team evolves on the fly, developing adaptability for real workplace challenges.

Norm-Setting
Teams develop comfort with iteration and course correction. The first time a boat sinks, people feel embarrassed. By the third failure, they're laughing, analyzing, and trying a new design. This shift from shame to curiosity is transformational. Teams learn that mistakes provide data, not proof of incompetence.

Transfer
Willingness to experiment, comfort with iteration, and ability to learn from failure transfer directly to workplace challenges. Teams that practice safe failure in games bring that mindset to product development, client problem-solving, and strategic planning.

Building Psychological Safety Through Shared Challenge
There's something remarkable about everyone facing the same difficult problem together: Hierarchies flatten and performance anxiety diminishes.

Here's why shared challenge creates psychological safety so effectively:

Vulnerability Becomes Normal
When everyone is figuring things out together, uncertainty stops feeling like weakness. The senior leader admits confusion about the next step. The newest team member offers a fresh perspective. Everyone struggles, making vulnerability the baseline rather than an exception to hide.

Competence Reveals Itself
Different people shine at different moments. The quiet person notices a crucial detail others missed. The one who typically dominates meetings gets stuck and needs help. Teams discover intelligence and

capability are more varied than org charts suggest. This realization that everyone has something valuable to contribute reshapes how teams operate when they return to work.

Mistakes Transform into Data
In typical work environments, mistakes carry professional risk. In problem-solving games, failures provide information for the next attempt. "That didn't work" becomes an observation rather than a judgment. Teams learn to treat setbacks as feedback rather than threats. This reframing may be the most valuable skill teams can develop—the ability to fail forward rather than retreat.

Success Belongs to Everyone
When the puzzle unlocks, the pipeline carries marbles end to end, or the boat crosses the finish line, the victory is collective. Nobody can claim solo credit. This shared achievement builds trust and reinforces collaboration in ways individual recognition never could.

Understanding why these activities work is valuable. Knowing how to amplify their impact is even better. Here are three methodologies facilitators and leaders can layer into any problem-solving activity—or apply directly in the workplace.

Advanced Problem-Solving Methodologies
Beyond running problem-solving activities, skilled facilitators and leaders can layer in methodologies that deepen learning and create stronger behavioral shifts. These approaches work during games and in real workplace settings.

The Plussing Technique
Pixar uses a creative process called "plussing" that transforms how teams handle ideas. Instead of traditional brainstorming where suggestions get shot down—"That won't work because . . ."—plussing requires every response build on the previous idea: "Yes, and we could also . . ."

This shift creates an additive rather than subtractive process. Ideas evolve through contribution, not criticism. During problem-solving activities, establish the rule that all suggestions must be acknowledged and built upon before being modified or replaced.

Watch what happens: people contribute more freely, combination ideas emerge that no one would have created alone, and the team develops a creative flow that feels effortless.

Plussing works because it removes the fear that kills innovation—the worry your idea will be dismissed. When people know their contribution will be considered and built upon, they share more. Teams practicing plussing during games instinctively carry it into meetings, brainstorming, and planning.

Devil's Advocate Protocol

Assign rotating roles where specific people question assumptions and challenge groupthink. This structure ensures critical thinking without turning negative:

- **The Questioner Asks:** "What if our basic assumption is wrong?" This forces teams to examine whether they're solving the real problem or just the most obvious version.
- **The Alternative Seeker Asks:** "What other approaches haven't we considered?" This prevents premature convergence and encourages exploration of better options.
- **The Consequence Tester Asks:** "If this approach fails, then what?" This builds contingency thinking and helps teams develop backup plans.

By making roles explicit and rotating them, teams avoid the friction of being "the one who always points out problems." Everyone takes turns, normalizing critical thinking and preventing any one person from being labeled negatively.

Role Reversal Problem-Solving

Have team members argue for approaches they don't prefer. The detail-oriented person argues for the broad-strokes approach. The risk-taker advocates for the cautious strategy. The individual contributor champions collaboration.

This technique expands empathy. When you must advocate for an approach you instinctively resist, you're forced to understand its merits. You discover legitimate reasons someone might prefer it. You see the problem from a different angle.

Teams practicing role reversal during problem-solving games develop a deeper understanding of how people think. The fast-moving entrepreneur learns why the careful analyst wants more data. The process-oriented manager understands why the creative designer resists structure. This perspective leads to more thoughtful decision-making in the workplace, where teams must balance competing priorities and preferences.

Creativity, Communication, and Trust Builders

Some of the most powerful team development happens through creative expression and improvisational thinking. These activities help teams adapt, support each other, and communicate under uncertainty—skills increasingly valuable in changing business environments.

Creative activities serve a different function than problem-solving challenges. Where problem-solving has clear success metrics and logical paths, creative collaboration focuses on:

- **Process over Product:** How teams navigate ambiguity and multiple "right" answers
- **Divergent Thinking:** Generating many possibilities rather than one solution
- **Risk-Taking:** Sharing ideas without knowing if they'll be well-received
- **Building on Others:** Using teammates' contributions as springboards
- **Embracing Imperfection:** Creating something "good enough" rather than perfect

The Improv Revolution: Core Improv Principles for Team Development

Jayne Hannah brings a unique perspective to team building from her background as a published playwright and improv expert. This is something we connected on the moment we met, and her insight summed it up perfectly:

"You can't script what we do. You've got to be able to adapt, listen, and react to your participants."

This adaptability is what modern teams need. Business environments change rapidly, customer needs evolve, and teams must pivot quickly while maintaining effectiveness and cohesion.

Agreement and Addition: Yes, and . . .

The foundational principle of improvisational theater has profound implications for team collaboration.

The Exercise

An introductory "Yes, and . . ." session begins by putting people into pairs. Each duo creates a scene by agreeing with and building on each other's contributions. Here's an example:

- **Partner A:** "The lunch today was great."
- **Partner B:** "Yes, and we got to eat two desserts!"
- **Partner A:** "Yes, and then I had tons of energy from all the sugar."
- **Partner B:** "Yes, and that's why we finished the project so quickly this afternoon!"

What Teams Experience

At first, many struggle. Their instinct is to say "yes, but . . ." or redirect the conversation or point out problems. Being forced to agree and build can feel unnatural. But as the exercise continues, ideas flow more freely. Scenes become more creative and fun. People start laughing together as the scenarios get more elaborate and unexpected.

Business Applications

How does this mindset change things? In meetings, instead of jumping to problems, team members build on ideas. During innovation sessions, ideas are developed further before evaluation. For conflict resolution, people find agreement before addressing disagreements. In change management, teams practice accepting new information and adapting rather than resisting.

Active Listening and Response: Pass the Clap

Most business communication—and most conversation—involves people waiting to speak rather than truly listening to understand and build on what others say. It develops coordination and communication skills through simplicity. And it's always a hit.

The Exercise

The team stands in a circle, facing each other. The goal is to pass a single clap around the circle as quickly and smoothly as possible. One person makes eye contact with the next and claps. That person receives the clap, makes eye contact with the next, and passes it along. The focus is on maintaining smooth flow and connection.

What Teams Experience

At first, the exercise feels awkward. People miss eye contact, clap at the wrong time, or hesitate. The flow breaks down and starts over. Some get frustrated with themselves or others. But gradually, things fall into place. The rhythm smooths out. Eye contact becomes natural. The clap moves around the circle, increasing in speed and fluidity. Teams often cheer when they achieve a full rotation without breaking the flow.

You can also add variations for extra skill building:

- **Adaptability:** Change direction mid-game
- **Coordination:** Add multiple claps circulating simultaneously
- **Multi-modal communication:** Include verbal sounds with claps
- **Performance under pressure:** Speed up gradually

Business Applications

Teams can apply these skills immediately. Nonverbal communication improves as teams learn to send and read clear signals. Timing and rhythm develop as groups build collective pacing. Recovery skills strengthen when mistakes happen and teams practice getting back on track. Attention and focus increase through awareness of both individual role and group dynamic.

Patience and Group Awareness: Count to 20

This exercise appears simple but requires sophisticated group coordination. It's a popular improv exercise, equal parts frustrating and entertaining, and it helps people notice subtle body language.

The Exercise

The group's challenge is to count from 1 to 20 without a predetermined order. If two people speak simultaneously, the group starts over. No signaling, gesturing, or "next in line" is allowed. Teams must develop organic awareness of when to speak and when to stay silent.

What Teams Experience

First attempts are chaotic, with multiple people jumping in at once, forcing restarts, or dead silent because everyone is afraid to mess up. Some try to dominate by speaking quickly, or others go silent, waiting for someone else to take initiative.

Eventually, teams realize success requires balance. Individuals must contribute while staying attuned to the group's energy. As patience develops, the count progresses, and some teams develop a pattern without needing to communicate or signal. When teams reach 20, the sense of accomplishment is palpable.

Business Applications

The lessons transfer to workplace dynamics. In meetings, teams become more aware of talking over each other and learn to create space for quieter voices. For project coordination, groups develop a better sense of timing and sequencing. In leadership development, natural leadership patterns become visible and can be discussed. For stress management, teams practice staying calm and focused when things don't go as planned, building resilience through repeated practice of starting over without blame.

Trust and Vulnerability: The Warm Fuzzies

This one uses positive recognition and appreciation to build trust and vulnerability. It's a favorite among facilitators thanks to its structured, safe format.

The Exercise

Everyone writes their name on a large envelope. Each team member writes "warm fuzzies" (positive notes) for everyone else. Notes should express genuine appreciation, things they've observed, or qualities they want others to know. When everyone finishes, each person receives their envelope of positive feedback to read privately or share with the group.

What Teams Experience

Some struggle at first with writing positive feedback, worried about being too effusive or not saying enough. It's often easier to write for some colleagues than others. But as the exercise continues, most find a rhythm. They recall specific moments when a colleague helped or showed a strength.

The notes become more thoughtful and specific. When people read their envelopes, the emotional impact is visible. Some tear up. Others smile. Many look surprised by what others noticed and appreciated.

Business Applications

The impact lasts beyond the exercise. Teams develop a positive focus, learning to notice and express their strengths rather than just spot problems. The structured format makes vulnerability feel safer than spontaneous praise. Quiet contributors often receive recognition they miss in day-to-day work.

What I love most about this one is knowing that many people keep these notes and revisit them during hard times, sometimes years later.

Advanced Communication: Party Quirks

This is another improv game I love because it builds observation, adaptability, and humor while fostering real team connection. It's used in drama education, professional improv, language classes, and even college parties—and it's incredibly effective for team building.

The Exercise

One person volunteers or is chosen as the host and temporarily leaves the room. Each remaining team member receives a unique quirk or character trait from the facilitator. Quirks can be characters ("thinks they're a superhero") or behaviors ("speaks only in questions" or "acts like everything is amazing").

When the host returns, the "party" begins. Guests enter one by one, acting out their assigned quirks. The host observes and tries to guess each quirk. The game continues until everyone's identified or time runs out.

What Team Experience

The host may feel overwhelmed trying to decode strange behaviors. Guests can feel self-conscious, but as they commit, they start having fun. The absurdity creates laughter. The energy builds as the host guesses correctly. Unidentified guests often exaggerate their quirks, making them easier to spot. The whole experience gets progressively sillier and more fun. By the end, even reluctant participants are laughing and engaged.

Business Applications

Hosts sharpen observation, learning to notice subtle cues and patterns. Guests grow in creative expression, conveying meaning through behavior rather than direct speech. Everyone practices flexibility, adapting to unexpected interactions.

Shared humor creates positive team bonds. Pattern recognition improves as teams learn to interpret indirect communication—a skill that translates directly to reading between the lines in business settings.

Creative Reframing: Excuses, Excuses

This creative and quick-thinking game helps teams practice reframing challenges and finding humorous perspectives under pressure.

The Exercise

One person acts as judge each round, presenting a scenario: "Why were you late to work?" "Why didn't you finish the report?" "Why is there a llama in the conference room?" Other team members take turns offering creative, funny, or outrageous excuses.

Excuses should be imaginative and entertaining, not believable. After everyone shares, the judge picks the most amusing or creative response. The winner becomes the next judge.

What Teams Experience

Some people freeze at first, worried their excuse won't be funny or creative enough. Others jump in with wild ideas. As rounds progress, people get more comfortable with the absurdity. Ideas become more creative and unexpected. "I was late because I had to teach a family of ducks to cross the road" becomes "I was late because I accidentally time-traveled to next Tuesday and had to wait four days to get back." The competitive element keeps energy high, but the tone stays playful. Even "losing" excuses get appreciation and laughter.

Business Applications

This game develops several valuable skills. Creative reframing helps people find positive or humorous takes on challenges, building resilience. Quick thinking improves as participants generate ideas rapidly without overanalyzing. Public speaking comfort grows through low-stakes presentations. Appreciation for creativity deepens as teams recognize and celebrate diverse thinking rather than just "winning" ideas. The low-pressure environment lets people experiment with new thinking styles.

Getting Past "I Could Never Do That"

Many team members resist creative or improvisational activities. They worry about looking foolish, not being artistic enough, or not understanding the "rules" of creative work.

Jayne addresses this resistance head-on: "Make it clear that this isn't about theater or telling jokes or performing sketches. It's about listening, good communication, and a sense of play and fun, and some confidence in yourself and how you react to things. There has to be very clear guidance on what's expected and a lot of coaching. You need a facilitator who recognizes it for the skill that it is and what it can actually do."

Strategies for Including Everyone

◆ **Focus on Skills, Not Performance:** Frame activities as practicing work-relevant skills (like listening, adapting, quick thinking) rather than performing.

◆ **Emphasize Process Learning:** We're not trying to be great at improv. We're practicing building on ideas instead of shutting them down.

◆ **Use Experienced Facilitation:** These activities require facilitators who understand both the craft and how to create psychological safety.

◆ **Start Small:** Begin with low-risk exercises and increase challenge as comfort grows.

The Intentionality Factor

The activities that grow teams aren't just about having fun, though the best ones are genuinely enjoyable. They're about creating shared experiences that develop the capabilities teams need to succeed in an increasingly complex and collaborative environment.

Problem-solving challenges can build resilience and adaptability. Creative collaborations help develop communication and trust. Purpose-driven service can create deeper bonds and shared meaning. The most effective team development activities combine strategic learning objectives with genuine human connection.

Every element should support specific team development goals: how instructions are delivered, how wins are celebrated, how lessons are processed afterward. With that level of purpose, activities stop being games and become transformational experiences teams carry forward.

Next, we'll explore something a bit different, but just as close to my heart: giving back.

CHAPTER 8

Giving Back Through Purpose-Driven Play

When we started offering charitable programs, I wondered if they'd work just as well or end up being a way for leaders to check a corporate social responsibility (CSR) box while coworkers volunteered together. The results were better than I ever imagined.

One time that stands out is the first time I watched a team assemble prosthetic hands—halfway through the assembly process, one participant suddenly stopped, looked at the hand he was working on, and said, "A real person who needs help is going to use these hands we're working on, so we need to make sure we come through for them. They're depending on us." The energy shifted, and people who'd been chatting suddenly focused, some even asking their teammates to quality-check their work.

Next came decorating the storage bags for these hands, and people started crying as they thought about who might use this hand and what they'd appreciate. It was such a moving experience, and this sort of thing happens regularly with events like this. This same team was still talking about this profound experience when we ran another program for them six months later.

Witnessing events like this convinced me that CSR activities are among the most valuable we run at TeamBonding. Something shifts when teams work together to help a cause they care about, and it goes deeper than what happens during other activities. They unite in a shared purpose that creates deeper bonds because they're making a real difference in the world.

The Triple Win Philosophy

Here at TeamBonding, I've come to refer to these charitable programs as triple-wins:

- ◆ **Win for the team:** Teams build stronger bonds, find shared accomplishments, and form lifelong memories.
- ◆ **Win for the company:** Brands improve their reputation, increase employee engagement, and align their actual actions with their stated values so they can walk the talk.
- ◆ **Win for the community:** Someone in need receives something they truly need—a prosthetic hand to restore independence, a bicycle that provides transportation to school or work, or a library box that serves the whole neighborhood, for instance.

This win-win-win makes CSR activities so valuable for today's companies. It also taps into a fundamental aspect of human psychology.

Why This Chapter Is Different

While traditional team building activities create shared experiences, CSR creates shared *meaning*, and that's a difference that changes everything. The activities in this chapter have all the benefits of the games from Chapter 7—building skills, forming connections, sparking confidence—but they do it through the lens of service, which changes everything.

When you're building a bike that a child will ride to school or a Little Free Library that will serve a neighborhood for years to come, everything changes. Creativity and quality become personal, and people zoom out to think about the world as a whole.

CSR activities differ from other games and events—they're not necessarily better, they just create a unique transformation. Teams usually remember and reference these activities the most because they know the people who benefited from their efforts are out there, living their lives a little better now. These are the experiences that change how people see the world, themselves, each other, and what they're capable of when they work together.

What You'll Discover

In this chapter, I'll share the signature CSR programs that consistently create profound impact for both teams and recipients. We'll explore:

- ◆ **The psychology of CSR** and why service creates deeper bonds
- ◆ **Signature CSR programs** that have transformed thousands of teams and lives
- ◆ **Design principles** for creating effective charitable experiences
- ◆ **How to choose programs** that align with your team's values

These aren't just volunteer activities with your coworkers—they use service as the vehicle for team transformation while improving brand reputation and helping the world—they're win-win-wins that I've come to cherish alongside my facilitators and thousands of participants who've tried them.

So, let's dive into the programs that prove you can do well by doing good, and that the best way to build a team might just be to build something together for someone else.

Signature CSR Team Building Programs

Of all the charitable team experiences we've developed, some consistently steal the show, creating profound impacts for teams and recipients alike. These experiences stand out for their unique ability to transform how teams see themselves and each other, and they do it while creating measurable, lasting change in communities.

All of these programs require genuine collaboration, and the effort your team puts forth directly impacts real people's lives. They also let teams see, touch, and hear about the difference they've made for others, which activates values that often remain dormant at work and brings out sides of people their colleagues may never have seen.

Teams remember these CSR experiences for years, and leaders rave not just about satisfaction but *transformation*. These aren't games by the standard definition of the word, but by tapping into compassion and creativity, many adults respond to these with laughter, joy, and a playful attitude.

Prosthetic Hands Project

What Teams Create: Prosthetic hands for amputees in developing countries

Shannon picked this program for inclusion in this section because it's her all-time favorite CSR option. She's seen how life-changing it can be for recipients and participants alike, and it always ends up moving people. It's one of my favorites as well, and it's hard not to tear up a bit every time we're wrapping up one of these events.

The Impact

Teams assemble prosthetic hands for hospitals and individuals in need around the world. Recipients gain the ability to eat, work, and live more independently.

"You're making gifts to give to the recipients and you can't match the freedom that these hands allow people—it's unbelievable," adds Shannon.

The Team Experience

- **Technical Challenge:** Assembly requires following precise instructions and quality control
- **Meaningful Stakes:** Everyone understands that real people will depend on their work
- **Skill Distribution:** Different team members contribute different capabilities (detail work, coordination, quality checking)
- **Emotional Connection:** Teams often receive photos and stories from recipients

Why It Transforms Teams

"The impact this project makes is unmatched," said Shannon. "When teams understand the life-changing impact—the freedom these hands provide for eating, working, and living independently—they tear up, and then they start to hold themselves and each other to higher standards in the best ways."

When everyone reaches the end of this event and fully grasps the impact they've made, facilitators and participants are often moved to tears. As another facilitator said: "Did you ever imagine that you'd have a job like this where if everyone cries, that's a good thing? That's success."

The combination of technical precision and emotional significance reveals the capacity for compassion and excellence in everyone who participates.

Just Roll With It (Skateboard Building)

What Teams Create: Skateboards for local children's charities or schools

This program combines hands-on construction with community impact for children who can't afford skateboards, and it's such a fun experience. It's one of Jayne's favorite CSR programs, and it always gets people excited when they find out what they're doing for the day.

The Impact

"There's a school in Dallas that we've done bikes, skateboards, and backpacks for," explains Jayne. "It means a lot for them because the families are from lower-income communities. The teachers are so passionate about these kids, and they've told us how much the families and children appreciate being seen in this way. These skateboards and stuff help give those kids confidence and connections that go beyond the classroom, and it makes a real difference in their lives. That means so much to me to hear, and I love getting feedback like this. It's inspiring."

Team members will design and assemble skateboards and decorate helmets for children in need, which are then donated to a school, like the one Jayne mentioned above, or a local children's charity.

The Team Experience

- ◆ **Project Management:** Coordinate multiple assembly lines and quality control processes
- ◆ **Resource Sharing:** Teams must manage materials efficiently across multiple skateboards

- **Standards Management:** Balance speed with quality when real safety is involved
- **Creative Collaboration:** Design custom graphics and decorations together
- **Time Pressure:** All boards must be completed and safety-tested within the time limit
- **Customization Opportunities:** Teams add personal touches that make each skateboard unique

Why It Transforms Teams

When teams know that real children will be riding these skateboards, quality becomes personal. Nobody wants to be the person who cut corners on a safety check. The combination of technical precision and creative expression brings out different strengths in team members. Some excel at following assembly instructions, others at artistic design, still others at quality control. Teams naturally organize themselves around these complementary capabilities.

The moment when teams see their completed skateboards lined up, decorated and ready to go, creates visible pride. These aren't abstract contributions, but tangible objects that teams can picture children riding. Many teams ask if they can meet the recipients or see photos of the kids with their skateboards later. That desire for connection reveals how invested they've become in creating something meaningful together.

The Charity Bike Build

What Teams Create: Bicycles for children around the world

These programs include a unique collaborative element that Shannon particularly loves. What starts as competition transforms into a living demonstration of how collaboration serves everyone better than isolated success, which is much more valuable.

The Impact

Teams build complete, functional bicycles that are donated to children in underserved communities. For many recipients, these bikes provide their first reliable transportation to school, after-school activities, or part-time jobs.

The Team Experience

- ◆ **Assembly Challenge:** Teams coordinate to build complete bicycles from components
- ◆ **Quality Standards:** Bikes must be fully functional and safe—recipients depend on them
- ◆ **Competitive Element:** Teams can earn points for completion speed and quality
- ◆ **Collaborative Twist:** Teams can also earn points by helping other struggling teams
- ◆ **Choice Points:** Continuous decisions about whether to focus on their own success or support others
- ◆ **Resource Management:** Sharing tools and expertise across team boundaries

Why It Transforms Teams

Shannon explains why this program stands out: "I love the events that are able to take away the competition and make things a bit more collaborative. Yes, we're helping the kids who are getting their bikes, but there's also an element woven in that's helping *each other*. Like, when another team is struggling with something or missing a part, you can earn points for your team by going and helping their team!"

That realization shifts the entire room. A lot of teams start the event focused solely on their own builds, intent on winning. But when another team starts to struggle, they're faced with a choice: keep racing ahead or lend a hand. Lending a hand is the more beneficial choice, so they usually choose to help, and the act of assisting another team strengthens trust across groups and redefines what success looks like.

This mindset tends to follow everyone back to the office. It helps people become more comfortable with looking out for one another and considering how they can lend a hand or what they can do for their coworkers. They realize that by helping everyone in the office, the company does better, their work performs better, and they do a better job.

Paws For a Cause
What Teams Create: Dog beds, dog toys, and cat scratch pads for local animal shelters

Perfect for animal-loving teams who want to help four-legged friends in need, this program creates beds, toys, and supplies for local animal shelters. There's something special about knowing your work will bring comfort to animals who've had difficult starts in life.

The Impact

Teams create multiple items including pet beds, toys, and supplies that are donated to local animal shelters. These items provide comfort and enrichment for animals waiting for their forever homes, making their shelter stay more bearable and increasing their chances of successful adoption.

The Team Experience

- **Task Variety:** Different projects require different skills (sewing, assembly, creative decoration)
- **Quality Matters:** Items will be used by real animals, so safety and durability are crucial
- **Immediate Visualization:** Teams can easily envision pets using their creations
- **Skill Distribution:** Team members gravitate toward projects that match their capabilities
- **Creative Expression:** Decoration and design allow for personality and fun
- **Empathy Development:** Understanding and discussing animal welfare needs

Why It Transforms Teams

The emotional connection here is immediate and universal. Even those who might not get excited about other charitable causes light up when they think about helping shelter animals. This shared affection creates instant common ground and natural collaboration. People who rarely interact at work start laughing together and helping each other out while they get hands-on with the project. They bond over a shared love of animals while they're sewing, stuffing, or assembling toys, and I've watched it create countless friendships.

When teams finally see the growing pile of finished beds and toys, the scale of their impact becomes real. I always hear things like, "Wow, no way, *we* made all of that?" Many want to visit the shelter, meet the animals, or find ways to continue supporting them, either by repeating this event, volunteering some other way, or sometimes adopting a pet! To me, this reveals how meaningful the experience is. It's not just team building—it's heart building.

Little Team Library (Partnership with Little Free Library®)

What Teams Create: Little Free Library® boxes for community spaces

Teams build and install book-sharing boxes that create ongoing community gathering points. This program stands out because unlike most team building activities, it creates permanent community infrastructure that will serve neighborhoods for years to come.

The Impact

Teams construct Little Free Library boxes that are installed in communities, joining a global network of more than 200,000 Little Free Libraries in 120+ countries on all seven continents (including one at the South Pole!). These libraries promote literacy, community connection, and the joy of discovering new books. As Scot Wirth from Little Free Library explains: "It creates a greater sense of community for the people living there. You stop, you look, you see what kind of books are in there. Someone else stops and leaves one. It's a wonderful cycle."

The Team Experience

- **Construction Collaboration:** Teams build the physical library structure together from provided materials
- **Design Decisions:** Choose colors, decorations, and placement strategies that reflect community character
- **Community Research:** Plan for optimal location and community engagement strategies
- **Creative Expression:** Decorate and personalize the library to make it welcoming

- **Long-Term Vision:** Consider how the library will integrate into community life over time
- **Installation Planning:** Coordinate logistics for permanent installation

Why It Transforms Teams

This program creates something lasting that teams can visit and show their families, which can change how they think about the lifespan of their work. It's not just about the day of the event, but about creating something that will serve the community long after they've gone home. That permanence inspires a different level of pride and investment.

This project requires a combination of strategy and creativity that draws out new strengths and helps unsuspecting people shine within their teams. You see natural planners, designers, and builders all finding ways to contribute, and this often highlights hobbies the group didn't know about before.

After the event, when they hear stories of children who were delighted to discover this library and find out they could have the book for free, their sense of accomplishment becomes deeply personal.

Many team members visit and contribute to their completed libraries weeks or months later, and they often bring family or friends to see what they made. That ongoing connection transforms what might have been a one-day activity into a shared legacy—a reminder of how collaboration, creativity, and community can build something that lasts.

Designing Effective CSR Experiences

Creating meaningful charitable team building requires more than good intentions. The most impactful experiences emerge from thoughtful design that balances community needs, team development objectives, and authentic values alignment. Over the years, We've identified four critical steps that separate transformational CSR programs from well-meaning activities that fall flat.

Step #1: Authentic Community Research

The most impactful CSR team building starts with a genuine understanding of community needs rather than imposed solutions.

Too many companies choose charitable activities based on what sounds good or what's convenient, without investigating whether communities actually want or need that contribution.

Best Practices

- **Partner with established local organizations** rather than trying to identify needs independently. These organizations already understand community challenges and have systems in place to distribute resources effectively.
- **Understand what communities actually want,** not what you assume they need. The difference matters. Your team might think a community needs one thing when residents would tell you something entirely different if you asked.
- **Research the track record and credibility** of potential charity partners. Not all charitable organizations operate with equal effectiveness or integrity. Due diligence protects both your team and the communities you aim to serve.
- **Verify that your contribution will genuinely make a difference.** Ask hard questions about how your work will be used, who will benefit, and what happens after your team leaves. If you can't get clear answers, keep looking.

Step #2: Structure for Collaboration

Design activities so success requires teamwork, not just individual contribution. The charitable nature of the work creates motivation, but the collaborative structure creates team development.

Effective Elements

- **Shared Goals:** Everyone works toward the same charitable outcome. This creates natural alignment and shared investment in quality and completion.
- **Resource Interdependence:** Teams must coordinate materials, time, or expertise. This prevents people from working in parallel without actual collaboration.
- **Quality Standards:** Real recipients depend on good work, creating mutual accountability. When teammates know

someone will use what they're building, they naturally hold each other to higher standards.

- **Role Differentiation:** Different people contribute different skills and capabilities. This allows team members to discover and appreciate diverse strengths.

Step #3: Connect to Company Values

Choose causes that align authentically with organizational mission and values. Forced alignment feels hollow to employees and risks creating cynicism rather than engagement.

Strategic Considerations

- **Mission Alignment:** How does this cause relate to what your company does or believes? The connection doesn't need to be literal, but it should feel genuine. A healthcare company supporting medical access makes sense. So does a tech company supporting digital literacy, or any company supporting education or community well-being.
- **Employee Resonance:** Will your team members genuinely care about this cause? Survey your team or look at what causes they already support individually. Authentic enthusiasm cannot be manufactured.
- **Skill Transfer:** Can people use or develop job-relevant skills while helping? The best CSR activities allow people to practice capabilities they need at work while serving the community.
- **Long-Term Potential:** Could this become an ongoing partnership rather than a one-time activity? Sustained relationships create deeper impact and more meaningful team connections than isolated events.

Step #4: Plan for Impact Visibility

Teams need to understand the difference they're making. Abstract contributions create abstract satisfaction. Visible, tangible impact creates lasting meaning.

Impact Communication Strategies

- ◆ **Recipient Stories:** Share photos and testimonials from people who benefit. Real faces and real stories make impact concrete and personal.
- ◆ **Quantified Impact:** Provide concrete numbers about lives affected. "We built 47 bikes for kids in underserved neighborhoods" means more than "We helped children."
- ◆ **Follow-Up Information:** Update teams on long-term outcomes when possible. A six-month update about how the Little Free Library is being used reinforces the lasting nature of their contributions.
- ◆ **Community Connection:** When possible, arrange for teams to meet recipients or beneficiaries. Direct interaction creates an emotional connection that transforms how people think about their work.

The Psychology of CSR

To understand why CSR has the impact it does, you have to look beyond the surface-level benefits of "doing good." Everyone at TeamBonding from Sales, to Marketing, to Accounting and Event Management have been deeply moved by what we've observed with these events.

Shannon captures this phenomenon beautifully:

"I've watched people step out of themselves when they're doing something charitable. The focus isn't on self-consciousness. Instead, it's on the end recipient and getting things together for that person, which changes everything. People automatically step away from their own needs and problems to look at the world from a new perspective, to think about someone else, and to consider how they can make an impact, which means so much to me.

"This sort of activity gets people out of their comfort zones because they feel like the focus isn't on them—it's on something else that they're contributing to, and they get to be part of making this incredible thing happen."

This sentiment echoes across countless team experiences.

"I agree with that, and I think it happens because there's a bigger sense of what they're doing together and how they're helping others that brings them together as a team," adds Jayne. "They're reminded that they're more than what happens in the office, and that they can work together to make things happen in big ways.

"This follows them back to the office and their daily tasks. Suddenly, they realize how much they've done for others, and it gives them confidence in their roles at work. It all stems from learning about how you can support others and what that feels like, and then translating it into your job with your team."

Why CSR Creates Transformation

This change in focus—from self to service—creates three fundamental shifts:

The First Shift: Identity Expansion

When teams do charitable work together, they expand their collective identity beyond *employees of Company X* to *people who make a positive difference in the world.*

"This sort of purpose-driven work is more about who I am as a person, who we are as a company in the community," says Jayne. "You're all learning about how you can support and give and what that feels like."

"It feels like the cherry on top of the shared purpose experience," adds Shannon. "Now all of a sudden you also feel like your crew has accomplished something together that made a legitimate, substantial difference. It's amazing."

This expanded identity changes how team members relate. Their shared compassion creates a bond they'll likely remember for the rest of their lives.

The Second Shift: Value Alignment

Volunteering activates a deep sense of meaning, tapping into values we share, and creating stronger emotional connections. Teams discover they care about similar causes, have similar definitions of meaningful work, and share similar visions for how they want to impact the world.

These discoveries create connection points that transcend hierarchies and departments, changing how people work together. When the executive and the intern both tear up during the prosthetic hands debrief, they share something profound. When two competitive sales teams collaborate during a bike build, they discover a new capacity for cooperation.

Value alignment is profound—it doesn't mean everyone believes in identical things, but that colleagues find enough common ground to build newfound trust and mutual respect.

The Third Shift: New Competencies

Many charitable activities require skills beyond those of each person's regular job. People don't just develop empathy; they're inspired to step up even when they're not experienced with something, getting out of their comfort zone and into a learning experience.

The graphic designer might discover a love of project coordination. The accountant might find a new artistic talent. The manager might be surprisingly good at detailed assembly work. Discovering these hidden capabilities serves multiple functions:

- **Increased Respect:** Team members see different sides of each other's capabilities, developing newfound respect.
- **Skill Transfer:** People discover hidden talents they can apply at work to better support their team, especially in cross-functional projects.
- **Collective Efficacy:** Teams realize they can handle anything that comes their way, building resilience and diversity for the organization.

When Service Becomes Your Competitive Advantage

Giving your team the opportunity to support a cause they're passionate about—to make a difference in the world—has the potential to fundamentally change how they operate. These events tend to access a new level of growth as they bond over shared values and the desire to help those in need.

Not where you're at right now? That's okay too. CSR isn't for every team or moment. Some teams first need to focus on basic communication and trust. Some companies need to get their own house in order before they can give back to others. If that sounds like you, you'll find no judgment from me. The ability to be honest about where you're at and what your team needs is an accomplishment in itself, and you know how I feel about checking boxes.

But if something in this chapter resonated and you found yourself thinking your team might be ready, I encourage you to pick a cause, schedule an event, and take action.

Your team has abilities you haven't fully discovered yet. They have a deep capacity for care, quality, and collaboration that might only surface when the work genuinely matters. They have the potential to be a team that makes a difference. Give them the chance to discover that by creating space in your company for genuine service. Watch what happens when purpose becomes your team's competitive advantage.

The prosthetic hands are waiting to be assembled. The bikes are ready to be built. The libraries are awaiting creation. Your team can be the one who helps. And in becoming that one, they'll become a different kind of team entirely.

That's the magic of the win-win-win. It's what happens when you stop asking "how do we build our team?" and start asking "what can we build together that matters?"

The answer might just transform everything.

Next, we'll explore something else that gives you the power to enact massive change: DIY team building you can do anytime, anywhere.

CHAPTER 9

DIY TeamBonding—Anywhere, Anytime

Don't have the budget for professional facilitators right away? That's okay! You can make magic happen on your own, too. Some of my favorite team building moments happened in window-less conference rooms with nothing but intentionality and enthusiasm.

It's what happens between people during an activity that actually makes team building work. It's the moment when two people realize they have the same weird hobby or when the quiet colleague suddenly takes charge. It's when a remote team finally laughs together in real time about something ridiculous.

Team building isn't about expensive props or elaborate setups. It's about authentic opportunities for people to see and appreciate each other, and I'm going to show you how to create these moments.

This chapter has everything you need: facilitator-tested activities that work in any environment, techniques for adapting professional approaches for DIY implementation, and the confidence to create meaningful team experiences regardless of constraints.

You can do this in an empty conference room, a virtual meeting, or even a casual lunch break.

I often suggest that regular TeamBonding clients try these approaches in the periods between their formal team building events—it helps get more from the journey they've started with their teams. But this isn't just for tight budgets or between-event maintenance.

These are powerful tools that work anytime, anywhere, with any team. Whether you're building your team building muscles between professional events or creating your first connection moments on a tight budget, this chapter will show you how.

Facilitator Favorites and High-Impact Options

We've run thousands of events in every conceivable setting with the facilitators at TeamBonding, and we've found several exercises that consistently deliver fun, engagement, and results regardless of circumstances. The instructions from these games come from Tyler Hayden, who has tested these as DIY exercises with countless leaders to great effect.

Minefield
Body/Kinesthetic; Visual/Spatial; Interpersonal

Time: 30–60 minutes | **Group Size:** 8–20+ | **Materials:** Mousetraps, eggs, stuffed toys, sponges, blindfolds

In this game, blind folded team members must walk through a zone covered with mousetraps, eggs, and stuffed toys, led by the voice of another team member. All the while, other members of the group will try to lead them off course and into "danger."

This is a fantastic way to demonstrate and practice communication skills.

Your Team Will

- ◆ Guide partners verbally through a task
- ◆ Learn to use appropriate motivators
- ◆ Practice verbal communication techniques
- ◆ Apply communication skills to the considerate treatment of others
- ◆ Realize varying "tenderness" and cultural differences

The Setup

1. **Set up a field:** Create clear start and finish zones. Place mousetraps (set them for added challenge), eggs, sponges, toys, and other obstacles along the course between the zones.

2. **Divide into pairs:** Split the team into pairs and ask each pair to pick a guide. It can be fun to have them play *Rock, Paper, Scissors* to decide randomly. Only one pair will be active at a time.

3. **Add distractions:** Assign some participants to serve as human distractions on the field. These can represent family, peers, project managers, customers, or competition. Their job is to attempt to verbally mislead the blindfolded participants. Rotate the distractions, with those who've already played taking the place of those who haven't.

4. **Place bumpers:** Have those who aren't actively navigating the course or serving as a distraction stand along the sides as bumpers, silently keeping the blindfolded participant from straying too far off-course.

How to Play

1. **Explain the rules:**
   a. The guides may only communicate verbally—their job is to guide their partner safely through the minefield.
   b. If the blindfolded person touches a mousetrap or obstacle, they must remove their blindfold and return to the beginning.
   c. Before they start again, the leader must first explain what they did well, what they could do better, and how they can apply these lessons for success in the future.
   d. **Optional:** The guide can lead their partner to pick up sponges and toys, which represent good decisions. Each time the blindfolded participant picks one up, ask them to identify one good decision they've made during the activity or one lesson they can apply to future projects.

2. **Pick the players:** Select the first pair to navigate the course. Have the guide stand at the end zone and the learner at the start zone.

3. **Start the game:** On the guide's signal, their partner will begin navigating the minefield to the finish zone without touching any mousetraps or eggs based on their verbal directions, all while ignoring distractions.

4. Rotate roles: Once the pair finishes, switch roles so the blindfolded participant becomes the leader to ensure everyone experiences both guiding and navigating.

Want to Increase the Challenge?

Consider asking participants if they would like to take off their shoes to cross the minefield. This would represent cultural differences and different levels of tolerance, because now the person could actually get hurt when their guide leads them astray.

Tell the participants to treat this person very tenderly and ask the leader how they will need to respond to their needs before they begin. This could yield some interesting debriefing points, but be careful and only add it if you feel your group is ready and everyone consents.

Sample Debrief Questions

- ◆ What did each thing represent (egg, mousetrap, distractions, etc.)?
- ◆ How did the distractions affect the person going through the maze?
- ◆ How can you more effectively communicate with the employee/team member/student?
- ◆ What other noises in life make it hard to communicate?
- ◆ What types of nonverbal communications may have helped?
- ◆ How did the person picking up the toys have to listen?
- ◆ How do you feel when you pick up a toy as a sender? A receiver?
- ◆ If you were communicating effectively, what would I see you doing?

Virtual Adaptation: This doesn't translate well to virtual settings. Instead, try a verbal-only navigation challenge where one person describes how to draw a shape or navigate a simple online maze while their partner can't see their screen.

Whadyesay?

Intrapersonal; Visual/Spatial; Mathematical/Logical; Verbal/Linguistic

Time: 15–25 minutes | **Group Size:** Pairs or small groups | **Materials:** Blank paper, pens, photocopy of geometric shapes graphic for the leader, "Supervising with Intelligence" handout, "7 C's of Communication" handout (from the appendix)

In this game, team members will pair up, with one attempting to get the other to duplicate a drawing. The trick is that only one person in each pair can see the drawing, and they must verbally communicate to the other what it looks like so that they can draw it on a piece of paper.

This helps team members expand their understanding and knowledge of communication.

Your Team Will

- ◆ Explore the communication process
- ◆ Express why multiple ways of communicating the same idea are often necessary to reach your cohort of direct reports

The Setup

1. **Prepare materials:** Photocopy the "Shapes and Such" graphic and the "7 C's of Communication" handout for each pair. You'll also need a blank sheet of paper and a pen for each pair.
2. **Arrange seating:** Set up seating so that each pair is far enough away from the others that they can easily communicate. The chairs should face the same direction so they're not looking at each other.

How To Play

1. **Pair up team members:** Divide the team into pairs. Ask them to decide who will be the listener and the speaker for their group.
2. **Explain the rules:** Tell them that the speaker will describe a series of shapes, and the listener's job is to draw a replica of what's being explained.
3. **Get ready:** Have the pairs sit in the chairs you set up earlier, with the speaker sitting behind the listener. Pass out a blank sheet of paper and a pen to the listeners, and the

photocopies of the "Shapes and Such" graphic and the "7 C's of Communication" handout to the speakers.

4. **Review time:** Give the speakers a moment to review the "7 C's of Communication."

5. **Start the clock:** Set a 15-minute timer and let the groups begin the activity.

6. **Evaluate the results:** When the teams have finished, have the listeners compare their drawings with the graphics their speaker described.

Want to Mix It Up?

Have the pairs switch roles—listeners becoming speakers, and speakers becoming listeners—and repeat the exercise. You'll either need to divide the four graphics provided or locate and print four new ones so the new listener doesn't know what to expect.

Sample Debrief Questions

♦ **Ask the listeners:**
   • What worked really well when your teammate was communicating with you?
   • What things did they say or do that helped you to recreate the graphic?

♦ **Ask the speakers:**
   • How did you apply the 7 C's of communication?
   • What could you have done differently when communicating with your teammate?
   • What are some of the things that you do best when you are communicating with others on your team?

Virtual Adaptation: This works perfectly in virtual settings. You can either pair up participants or have everyone draw the shapes on their screen while you describe the shapes, and have participants draw along.

Scarecrow

Body/Kinesthetic; Visual/Spatial; Interpersonal; Verbal/Linguistic

Time: 40–70 minutes | **Group Size:** 8–20 | **Materials:** Blindfolds, hay bale (or fabric scraps), long sleeve shirt, pants, hat, boots, chair, belt, cordage, work gloves, safety scissors, small burlap bag, cue cards, tape/stick pins

In this game, your group will wear blindfolds and build a scarecrow out of provided supplies. Once complete, they'll accessorize the scarecrow with items chosen as metaphors for skills that good communicators often use.

Teams will strengthen communication and listening skills.

Your Team Will

- ◆ Talk about specific communication skills each person used effectively
- ◆ Practice communicating with their colleagues
- ◆ Be involved in a task that stretches their current communication skills
- ◆ Practice verbal and nonverbal communication skills

The Setup

1. **Prep your materials:** Get your materials ready in the room ahead of time. You'll pass them out to the group, so you simply need to have them close at hand.
2. **Discuss communication:** Spend about 5 minutes discussing how being an effective communicator enables people to do their job more effectively and efficiently. Ask:
   a. What is communication?
   b. When do we do it?
   c. How?
3. **Prompt responses:** Have each person finish this statement: "When I'm being an effective communicator, you see me . . ."

How to Play

1. **Ready your players:** Have the group sit in a circle and ask everyone to put on blindfolds.
2. **Explain the directions:** Ask them to listen carefully because you're only explaining the directions once—this game is meant to highlight how important listening is in the communication loop.
   a. You will pass out one item to each person: hay bale, long sleeve shirt, pants, hat, boots, chair, belt, cordage, work gloves, safety scissors, and small burlap bag.
   b. The group has 15 minutes to build a scarecrow using the materials provided.
   c. When completed, they'll take off their blindfolds and accessorize the scarecrow.
3. **Start the blindfolded phase:** Following the directions you explained earlier, pass out items and start the timer. If your team is struggling too much, allow each person to remove their blindfold for 15 seconds to get an idea of what they're working with. If this doesn't help enough, have them complete the task sighted.
4. **Celebrate:** At the end of the 15 minutes, have everyone remove their blindfolds and celebrate their successful construction before moving on.
5. **Accessorize:** Ask participants to dress the scarecrow in metaphors that convey the attributes of a great team communicator. Provide blank cue cards to write their "tag" and tape or stick pins to put them on the scarecrow after explaining their item. Examples:
   a. Sunglasses = Cool under pressure
   b. Fancy shoes = Expresses professionalism
   c. Reading glasses = Can focus on fine details

Sample Debrief Questions

- ◆ How did wearing a blindfold force you to communicate?
- ◆ Who was communicating well? What specifically were those people doing that made them effective communicators?

- When did you communicate well verbally and nonverbally? How? Why? With whom?
- When did you listen well? Why? How were people communicating that encouraged you to listen that way?
- How do you know when others have received what you communicated effectively?
- Where does planning come into play for good communication of activities and projects?
- What are 3 ways to effectively communicate an upcoming project?
- How did people encourage feedback from the group?

Virtual Adaptation: Skip this one for virtual teams. The physical, tactile nature is what makes it work. Try "Whadyesay?" instead for virtual communication skill building.

Nuclear Reactor

Visual/Spatial; Interpersonal; Body/Kinesthetic; Mathematical/Logical

Time: 30–45 minutes | **Group Size:** 8–20 | **Materials:** Kite string (four meters per person), rubber band, two cups, tennis ball

In this game, team members will rebuild a structure of cups and a tennis ball using only strings attached to a rubber band. The activity creates different constraints of time and relationship that highlight the importance of situational leadership as conditions change.

Your team will explore how different situations require different leadership approaches and practice adapting their style accordingly.

Your Team Will

- Use different styles of leadership
- Demonstrate leadership and "followership" roles
- Apply situational leadership to their role as leader
- Observe the effects of different situational leadership roles

The Setup

1. **Prepare the equipment:** Cut kite string into 4-meter lengths, one per learner. Tie all the strings to one rubber band at equal intervals like spokes on a wagon wheel.
2. **Create the reactor:** Place two cups together in the center of the teaching space with a tennis ball inside one cup.
3. **Position the crane:** Lay the rubber band and strings beside the cups with the strings radiating outward.
4. **Set the atmosphere:** Dim the lights (black lights create a dramatic effect).

How to Play

1. **Set the scene:** Meet learners outside the "reactor room." In a distinguished voice, welcome them to "Homer Simpson's Nuclear Power Generation & Donuts" and explain they're touring the facility to see the pride and joy reactor, "Spooo."
2. **Tour the reactor:** Point out the reinforced nuclear reactor (cups), radioactive material (tennis ball), and nuclear crane (rubber band with strings). Explain that each extending handle represents an individual team member.
3. **Create the crisis:** As you're leaving for tea, "accidentally" trip and spill the reactor, scattering the contents. Immediately, the containment system locks down and announces: "The system has experienced failure in the main Spooo generator. Total containment required in three minutes. Rescue crews must utilize the crane to reconstruct the reactor."
4. **Start the clock:** Give the team only 3 minutes to rebuild the structure using the crane. Keep pressure on by announcing time remaining.
5. **Celebrate or retry:** When time expires, acknowledge their effort regardless of completion.

Round Two—Shift the Leadership Style

1. **Remove time pressure:** Give the group as long as they need to rebuild the structure.
2. **Observe the shift:** Note how eliminating time constraints changes how they interact and lead.
3. **Allow completion or strategic pause:** Let them achieve success or, if they're extremely frustrated and consent, offer to revisit later.

Want to Increase the Challenge?

After the first round, require that participants can only touch their own string and cannot speak to each other during the rebuild.

Sample Debrief Questions

After Round One (Task Leadership):

◆ How does time pressure necessitate a different style of leadership?
◆ What did you do effectively to get the job done?
◆ What's the difference between leadership and followership? Why are both required in time-pressured situations?
◆ How did you decide who would lead? Was there time for collaboration and democratic process?
◆ What should a leader do after using this style to ensure continued team engagement?

After Round Two (Maintenance Leadership):

◆ What's the difference in team functioning when the leader has time to collaborate?
◆ How do you feel about the outcome when you're part of solution-building? How is that different from task-related situations?
◆ When is this leadership style appropriate in a project lifecycle?
◆ How do people's professional competencies play into this style of leadership?

Virtual Adaptation: This can work virtually with a digital simulation where team members control different "strings" on a shared screen, or use a collaborative drawing tool where each person can only move certain elements.

Frog Pond

Visual/Spatial; Naturalistic; Body/Kinesthetic; Interpersonal

Time: 30–45 minutes | **Group Size:** 10–40 | **Materials:** Soft toys/stuffed animals, stepping stones (one per two participants minus 1–2), boundary markers for field

In this game, half your team (frogs) attempts to cross a defined area (pond) using stepping stones while the other half (rascals) throws soft toys (rocks) at the frogs. Each group must work collaboratively to realize their objectives—either hitting frogs or safely crossing to the other side.

Your team will investigate leadership and collaboration as both groups work toward opposing goals.

Your Team Will

♦ Explore personal leadership approaches
♦ Explore the benefits of collaboration
♦ Complete a task requiring both leadership and collaboration
♦ Apply leadership and collaboration to their roles within their work team

The Setup

1. **Build the playing field:** Create a 15-meter by 5-meter rectangular area using cones or markers.
2. **Gather materials:** Collect soft toys and enough stepping stones for half your group minus one or two (e.g., 20 participants = 9 or 8 stepping stones).

3. **Divide the team:** Split the group in half—one half becomes frogs, the other becomes rascals.
4. **Position teams:** Frogs start at one end of the pond, rascals position along the 15-meter sides.

How to Play

1. **Explain the rules:**
   a. Frogs must travel collectively from start to finish using only the lily pads (stepping stones).
   b. Frogs are only safe when touching lily pads or behind start/finish lines.
   c. Rascals throw stones (soft toys) at frogs, trying to hit them below the waist when they're not on lily pads.
   d. If a frog gets hit, the entire group returns to the beginning.
   e. Rascals can move up and down the 15-meter sides to improve their aim.
   f. All frogs must move collectively—no one crosses alone.
2. **Establish the metaphor:** Explain that "stones" represent obstacles to success (poor communication, lack of planning, insufficient resources), "rascals" represent blockers or naysayers, "frogs" represent the work team, and the "pond" represents the project timeline.
3. **Start the activity:** Let the frogs strategize briefly, then begin.
4. **Switch roles:** After completion or multiple attempts, have frogs become rascals and vice versa.

Want to Increase the Challenge?
Remove one or two more stepping stones, require frogs to transport an object across the pond, or add a time limit.

Sample Debrief Questions

◆ What did the frogs and rascals do before the first step across the pond?
◆ How did the frogs work together to achieve success?

- Who was the leader? Were they always the leader? Did anyone else lead?
- What special skills did each frog bring to crossing the pond?
- How do special skills help a group achieve success?
- How do people feel when a collaborative group works well?
- What is collaborative leadership and how did you just demonstrate it?
- What are the benefits of collaborative leadership?
- What does your group need to know about itself to collaborate well?
- What needs to happen before working together to create space for collaborative leadership?

Virtual Adaptation: Create a simple online game where half the team navigates through a virtual maze while the other half places obstacles. Use platforms like Miro or shared screens with drawing tools.

Bannuka

Visual/Spatial; Interpersonal; Body/Kinesthetic; Mathematical/Logical

Time: 40–60 minutes | **Group Size:** 6–15 | **Materials:** M&M's or other candy currency, craft supplies (popsicle sticks, glue, markers, cardboard, construction paper, small boxes, scissors, yarn, etc.), price list, toy car or small object

In this game, team members work in small teams to build a carrier or display case for a toy car. They must allocate resources wisely and trade for supplies using candy currency while being charged labor costs every five minutes. Teams explore project planning and resource allocation to complete their task.

Your team will experience skills that enable them to become more effective planners with limited resources.

Your Team Will

- ◆ Create a mission for their team
- ◆ Explore how to manage resources effectively to reach their mission
- ◆ Maintain dialogue about integrating good planning into their project and leadership experience
- ◆ Perform evaluation both formatively and summatively

The Setup

1. **Prepare the marketplace:** Display all craft supplies on a table with price tags (in M&M units).
2. **Create the price list:**
   a. 30 popsicle sticks = 40 M&M's
   b. Cup of glue = 15 M&M's
   c. Leasing markers = 10 M&M's per 10 minutes
   d. 8.5 × 11 cardboard = 50 M&M's
   e. 3 sheets construction paper = 10 M&M's
   f. Small cardboard box = 25 M&M's
   g. Scissors = 5 M&M's per 10 minutes
   h. Labor = 5 M&M's per 5 minutes
   i. Additional items as desired
3. **Prepare currency:** Give each team a bag of M&M's (ensure equal distribution).
4. **Arrange seating:** Have teams sit together in planning areas.

How to Play

1. **Introduce Bannuka:** Welcome them to "Bannuka, the ancient Nova Scotian art of trading." (Feel free to create an entertaining backstory about its origins.)
2. **Explain the project:** Their task is to design and build a carrying case large enough to fit their toy car (or alternative: team memory box, donation item, etc.).

3. **Establish the rules:**
   a. M&M's are the currency for this activity
   b. All building materials must be purchased from the market-place at listed prices
   c. Labor charges: Every 5 minutes after their first 5 minutes of planning, they'll be charged 5 M&M's
   d. They can only use supplies from the marketplace—no outside materials
   e. Leftover M&M's can be eaten after completion!
4. **Create the mission statement:** Guide them through creating a mission statement (under 100 words) that answers:
   a. What function will you perform as a group?
   b. For whom do you perform this function?
   c. How do you go about performing this function?
   d. **Example:** "The Honey Suckers is an efficient and effective planning and development group who builds appropriate parking structures for soap box racers in a timely manner to meet external and internal expectations."
5. **Start planning time:** Give them 5 minutes to plan their approach and determine what supplies they'll need.
6. **Collect labor charges:** After the initial 5 minutes, collect 5 M&M's every 5 minutes for continued labor.
7. **Begin construction:** Allow them to purchase supplies and build their carrier.
8. **Celebrate completion:** When teams finish (or time expires), celebrate their work and let them enjoy remaining M&M's!

Want to Increase the Challenge?
Add unexpected "expenses" like inspection fees, require specific design features (roof, windows), or introduce material shortages halfway through.

Sample Debrief Questions

- ◆ What process did you go through when planning to build the structure?
- ◆ How did you allocate resources so the job was completed efficiently and effectively?

◆ How did you know what the structure should look like? (Benchmarking from similar structures?)

◆ What are the most successful projects you've been involved in? What made them effective?

◆ How do you decide who does what?

◆ How do you ensure the job is getting done?

◆ What do you do when the project is finished to define closure?

Virtual Adaptation: Use virtual currency (points) and have teams "purchase" digital tools or features for a collaborative online project (creating a shared presentation, designing a virtual space, etc.). Track their budget in a shared spreadsheet.

Knot Fun

Interpersonal; Visual/Spatial; Body/Kinesthetic

Time: 40–90 minutes | **Group Size:** 6–20 | **Materials:** Long rope with multiple knots tied in it (approximately 1 meter per 3–4 people)

In this game, team members hold onto different sections of a knotted rope with one hand and cannot move their grip. Working together without letting go, they must untie all the knots in the rope. This challenge explores the interpersonal resources required for successful issue resolution.

Your team will experience the collaborative problem-solving skills needed when everyone is connected to the same challenge.

Your Team Will

◆ Identify the need to ask for help from others

◆ Discuss how to maximize the resources of people around them

◆ Create opportunities to aid each other in resolving issues

◆ Discuss the benefits of helping someone achieve success in issue resolution

◆ Create a methodology to resolve issues

◆ Achieve success in resolving an issue

The Setup

1. **Prepare the rope:** Take a rope approximately 1 meter long for every 3–4 participants. Tie overhand knots at regular intervals along the rope.
2. **Calculate knot placement:** Ensure that when each person holds the rope with one hand, they have a knot on their left and right (except end people, who have one knot on the inside).
3. **Brief the team:** Explain that resolving issues takes practice and awareness of many external factors. Share a brief example of an issue you or someone resolved in a similar work context.

How to Play

1. **Position participants:** Ask the group to pick up the rope with one hand (whichever is more comfortable) between the knots. End people will only have a knot on one side.
2. **Establish the constraint:** Tell them their hands are "stuck fast" to the rope and cannot be moved from that position.
3. **Present the challenge:** Without removing their hands, the group must untie all knots in the rope.
4. **Introduce the metaphor:**
   - The rope represents a program or responsibility they're all involved in
   - The knots represent issues encountered in creating a strong project (knots reduce rope strength!)
   - Not letting go represents everyone's commitment to effective project completion
5. **Begin the challenge:** Let them work through untying the knots.
6. **Add extra challenge (optional):** If they complete it quickly, have them tie a new knot in the center of the rope without letting go!

Want to Increase the Challenge?
Require participants to use only one hand throughout, add more knots, or work in complete silence.

Sample Debrief Questions

- What was the first thing you did as a group to decide how to untie the knots?
- What role did you play in untying the knots? Why did people play different roles?
- How can you apply untying knots to the collective projects you need to do?
- What were the specific things you did to solve the issue and in what order?
- What generalizations about issue resolution can you make using the specifics you identified?
- Name three things you need to do to resolve issues as a team.

Virtual Adaptation: This doesn't translate well virtually. Instead, try a collaborative problem-solving challenge using a shared digital workspace where each person controls only one element needed to complete the solution (like a virtual escape room).

Blindfold Maze

Visual/Spatial; Interpersonal; Body/Kinesthetic

Time: 30–40 minutes | **Group Size:** 6–20 | **Materials:** Long rope, blindfolds for all participants, trees or posts to tie rope to

In this game, blindfolded team members must find their way out of a circular maze made of rope. The only solution is asking for help from the facilitator. This activity powerfully demonstrates that asking for support from others helps ensure effective and efficient conclusions to challenges.

Your team will experience why reaching out for help is a crucial resource in issue resolution.

Your Team Will

- Identify the need to ask for help from others
- Discuss the idea of multiple resolutions to issues
- Create opportunities to aid each other in resolving issues
- Discuss benefits of helping someone achieve success
- Create a methodology to resolve issues

The Setup

1. **Choose the location:** Select a level area free of protruding rocks and roots.
2. **Create the maze:** Tie rope from point to point (tree to tree or posts), creating a closed circle with no opening.
3. **Clear the area:** Remove any sticks or rocks from inside the maze.
4. **Prepare participants:** Blindfold learners in a location where they cannot see the maze setup.

How to Play

1. **Form a line:** Have blindfolded participants hold hands to create a connected line.
2. **Give safety instructions:** Tell them they'll take a brief walk requiring total silence so they can hear your directions. Remind them to respect and support each other for safe arrival.
3. **Lead to the maze:** Safely walk the group to the maze and position them inside at various points around the circle so they don't readily run into one another.
4. **Position on rope:** Have each person hold onto the rope at their position.
5. **Explain the scenario:** With participants standing still, say: "The rope you're holding represents your timeline to personal success. Currently, you're all holding a different point within the project because everyone has different skill levels and starting positions. This timeline follows a path leading to project completion—the exit from the maze. You must successfully complete the project. However, if you need help finding successful completion, all you have to do is ask for

'help' and someone will support you. You must continue wearing the blindfold as it represents the uncertainty of what comes next—it's hard to anticipate everything in a project. Are there any questions?"

6. **Begin the activity:** Let learners try to find the way out.
7. **Respond to requests:** When someone asks for "help," walk directly to them, remove their blindfold, motion for them to be quiet, and guide them under the rope. Have them sit aside or help you remove others.
8. **Continue until complete:** Keep going until everyone is out of the maze.

Want to Increase the Challenge?

Make the circle larger, add obstacles inside the circle that participants must navigate around, or have removed participants provide hints (but not direct instructions) to those still in the maze.

Sample Debrief Questions

- How did it feel to be stuck in the maze?
- What strategies did you try before asking for help?
- How did empowering others to help you change the situation?
- What are the benefits of helping others versus completing tasks independently?
- When is asking for help important in your work?
- How do you create an environment where people feel comfortable asking for help?
- How can you make it easier for team members to reach out for support?
- What's the difference between asking for help and delegating?
- How do you follow up with people when they help you?

Virtual Adaptation: Create a text-based puzzle or riddle where participants work individually in breakout rooms. The only way to solve it is by asking the facilitator for a specific clue in the main room. Track who asks for help and when.

Mammoth Monument
Visual/Spatial; Interpersonal; Verbal/Linguistic

Time: 30–60 minutes | **Group Size:** 10–50 | **Materials:** Personal objects from participants, structure to attach items to (wooden chair, plywood, tree section, fabric), attachment supplies (nails, glue, tape, string, pins)

In this game, each team member brings an object that represents a positive quality they possess. One by one, they introduce themselves, explain their object's significance, and attach it to a shared structure, creating a monument that represents the unique contributions of the entire team.

Your team will create a physical icon that represents the group's collective identity and individual strengths.

Your Team Will

- ◆ Experience working as a group toward a common goal
- ◆ Identify personal attributes that contribute effectively to achieving group goals
- ◆ Examine how to communicate within a large group

The Setup

1. **Prepare the base structure:** Set up a wooden chair, plywood sheet, tree section, or fabric on a stand that can support objects being attached to it.
2. **Gather attachment materials:** Have available nails, glue, tape, string, and pins for participants to affix their objects.
3. **Arrange the space:** Position the base structure in a central location where everyone can gather around it.

How to Play

1. **Introduce the concept:** Explain that each project team has the opportunity to be individual and spectacular because each member brings different attributes—no two teams have the same makeup.

2. **Request objects:** Ask individuals to pull out an object they brought that represents who they are. Examples:
   - Broken clock = Always late but eventually arrives
   - Teddy bear = Provides comfort and support
   - Work glove = Gets the job done when needed
   - Keys = Opens doors to new solutions

3. **Establish the process:** Each individual will:
   - State their name
   - Describe their object
   - Explain why it represents a positive quality they bring to the monument/team

4. **Sample presentation:** "Hi, my name is Tyler Hayden, and this is my favorite work glove because when push comes to shove, you can always count on me to get the job done."

5. **Attach objects:** After introducing their object, each person affixes it to the structure using the available materials.

6. **Name the monument:** When everyone has placed their object, the group collectively names their monument.

7. **Display with pride:** Place the completed monument in a place of honor where all can see it.

Want to Increase the Challenge?

Have participants attach their objects in a way that structurally supports the next person's object, requiring more planning about order and placement.

Sample Debrief Questions

- How did it feel to share something personal about yourself?
- What surprised you about what others shared?
- Why is it important that everyone be seen and heard?
- What role does each person play in completing a group task? What happens when one is missing?
- How will you function within this large group moving forward?
- How can you maximize everyone's individual strengths?
- How does this monument represent your team's identity and variety of capabilities?

- How will you refer back to these individual strengths as you work together?
- What commitment are you making to each other by building this monument together?

Virtual Adaptation: Use a collaborative digital platform (Miro, Jamboard, or PowerPoint) where each person adds an image or icon representing their quality, along with their name and explanation. Create a digital collage that can be saved and referenced throughout the project.

Beyond the Basics: Advanced DIY Techniques

You officially have several activities you can use right away. But how do you turn these games into transformational experiences?

There are techniques that professional facilitators spend years developing, and while you won't be perfect at them without practice, you can learn the fundamentals right here, right now.

The difference between *making* your team do an activity and getting them *excited* comes down to three core competencies:

- Reading your team's energy so you can adjust in real time
- Managing transitions and resistance with grace
- Creating psychological safety through intentional design choices

Master these, and you'll create experiences they'll be talking about for months.

Reading the Room: Energy Assessment and Management

Monitoring the group's energy and knowing when to adjust activities take practice and skill. Facilitators watch for body language, engagement, and conversations as activities progress. Depending on what they observe, they'll often change things up to address any issues.

The following quick guide can help you do this for your own activities.

Energy Indicators to Watch

Here are some of the most important things to look out for with your team and what to do when you see these indicators pop up.

Physical posture:
- Slouching = low energy or disengagement
- Leaning back = skepticism or withdrawal
- Looking away = distraction or discomfort
- Leaning forward = engagement and interest

Example Solution: I once noticed an entire team slouching before a big meeting, so I switched things up with a game of Minefield. After the game, everyone was laughing and more energized.

Participation patterns:
- Who's contributing consistently and who's checking out?
- Do contributions feel genuine or obligatory?
- Are people building on each other's ideas or just waiting for their turn?
- Do you see engaging sidebar conversations happening, or do people seem scattered?

Example: "I ran a virtual event with 600 people, and the energy was completely scattered," says Jayne. "People weren't engaging, and you could just feel the overwhelm. We immediately pivoted to break-out rooms of 15–20 people. Within minutes, conversations started flowing and energy shifted from scattered to engaged."

Conversation flow:
- Natural discussion that flows easily vs. forced responses
- Laughter and spontaneity vs. polite silence
- Questions from participants vs. silence after your prompts
- Cross-talk and interruptions (good sign!) vs. one person speaking at a time

Example: "I once watched a leadership team try to force participation in a sociable event by saying, 'Come on, now's the time to ask questions!' The more they pushed, the quieter the room became. That's when I knew we needed to pivot to a low-pressure activity like 'Whadyesay?' where people could engage without feeling put on the spot," Jayne recalls. "Ten minutes later, people were more open to asking questions about the main event."

Movement quality:
- Energetic vs. sluggish participation in physical activities
- Quick transitions vs. dragging feet between activities
- Genuine engagement with materials vs. half-hearted participation
- Restlessness vs. stillness

Example: "I worked with one group whose responses were sluggish and half-hearted," says Shannon. "As soon as I got them to stand up and form a circle for a game, something shifted. You could see the energy change—people were moving with purpose, making eye contact, and engaging. That simple transition from sitting to standing literally changed the room."

More Energy Adjustment Examples

- **Low energy?** Use physical activities like Minefield and Frog Pond to amp it up.
- **Energy scattered?** Use focus activities like the Knot Fun to help people zero in.
- **Anxious vibes?** Use structured games like Bannuka to help people relax.
- **Resistant attitudes?** Use low-pressure activities like Whadyesay to ease people in.

The Art of Seamless Transition
Moving from work into team building activities calls for finesse and intentionality. The following are two important skills that'll help you pull it off.

Skill #1: Effective openings

Lead with the energy you want to see throughout the activity. This means practicing your openings so you can kick things off with the right vibe. Here are some examples of how my top facilitators handle things:

- "Before we dive in, let's take five minutes to connect as humans."
- "We're coming up on some challenging topics, so let's have a bit of fun together before we get started."
- "I know everyone's coming from different meetings and mindsets, so I have a fun game to help everyone get on the same page."

The key is acknowledging the transition and easing into it instead of hitting everyone with a sudden announcement or jarring change.

Skill #2: Clear instructions

Unclear instructions are frustrating and leave everyone confused. Here's how to nail it:

1. **Get attention first:** Don't start explaining until everyone's focused on you.
2. **Explain the why:** Give a sentence or two of context about why you're doing the activity.
3. **Give simple directions:** Deliver short and sweet instructions you rehearsed ahead of time. Try to keep it under a minute.
4. **Demonstrate when possible:** Show, don't tell. Demonstrate physical activities with a volunteer instead of just talking.
5. **Check for understanding:** Ask if anyone has questions they want to clear up ahead of time, but don't sound condescending.

Handling Resistance and Reluctance

Some people initially resist building activities due to past negative experiences. The following are some common types of people you might encounter and how to address each one:

The Eye-Roller

These are the team members who visibly signal skepticism or disdain. You'll see things like crossed arms, heavy sighs, and the dreaded dramatic eye roll. They're often influential team members, and their visible resistance can spread.

- **Don't call them out:** Public confrontation increases resistance and creates uncomfortable dynamics. Instead, try something like: "I'm sure some of you are skeptical, and that's okay! You don't have to participate if you don't want to."
- **Start with less-silly activities:** Skip games like Nuclear Reactor initially and try options such as Whadyesay that feel more like conversations than games.
- **Give skeptics a role:** Make them the timekeeper, observer, or judge. Contributing without participating often leads to gradual buy-in as they watch others engage positively.

The Non-Participant

These are the quiet observers who simply don't engage. They're not visibly resistant, just absent from participation.

- **Make participation optional:** Try leading with something like, "Everyone's invited to participate, but it's also okay to observe if that's more comfortable for you today." Sometimes having the option triggers buy-in.
- **Offer different ways to contribute:** Some who feel they can't speak up in groups might have an easier time writing/texting. Others will participate in pairs but not in large groups. Design multiple participation pathways into every activity.
- **Check in privately:** Sometimes non-participation signals cultural differences, negative experiences, or personal circumstances. A quiet "Hey, you seem like you might be holding back—is everything okay?" often reveals helpful information.

The Over-Enthusiast

These team members dominate activities, talk over others, and sometimes overwhelm quieter teammates with their energy.

- **Channel their energy into helping others:** Redirect enthusiasm productively with something like, "You're crushing this activity! Can you help me with the groups that are struggling?"
- **Give them leadership roles within activities:** Make them group leaders or activity explainers for others to use their energy while distributing attention more evenly.
- **Set gentle boundaries to help quieter teammates:** "Let's make sure everyone gets a chance to share before anyone goes twice," or "I love your enthusiasm! Can you help me bring out some of the quieter voices?"

Troubleshooting Common DIY Challenges

Facilitators must also handle the unexpected with grace. Sudden obstacles or objections from your team can be intimidating, but here are a few common challenges and how to address them:

"I Don't Have Enough Time!"

This is the most common challenge people encounter. Let's look at it from a few angles. First, you can always ease in with regular icebreakers from Chapter 6 before moving up to scheduling longer games like these:

- Whadyesay? (15–25 minutes)
- Frog Pond (30–45 minutes)
- Nuclear Reactors (30–45 minutes)

Even 30 minutes of authentic connection beats 90 minutes of disengagement. Quality over quantity!

It also helps to shift the perspective so people stop thinking of team building as separate from work. These are productivity detractors; they're investments in relationships and skills that improve productivity. Implementing team building into existing structures might help with this. Alternatively, check out the appendix for additional energizers you can use to ease into team building games.

"My Team Is Too Serious!"

Lots of people think their team is too serious to enjoy games. Try reframing the approach with these perspective shifts:

- Call activities "skill builders" or "connection exercises" rather than "games"
- Emphasize the business benefits like communication, collaboration, and innovation
- Start with less playful activities and ease into games later
- Model participation as the leader to encourage them to mirror your engagement

"We Don't Have Space to Move Around!"

Many people assume they simply can't overcome this one, but a small space can offer great results because everyone is collectively working to overcome the same challenge. Still, I suggest sticking with seated options like these so you can focus on fun:

- Whadyesay can be done seated
- Knot Fun can work in small space
- Mammoth Monument can be done in small spaces

"Remote/Hybrid Teams Are Too Complicated!"

A lot of the facilitators at TeamBonding were worried about transitioning to remote formats when lockdown hit, but it was amazing and we made adjustments that improved several programs. I included virtual adaptations in the book this very reason. Here are some tips for working with both formats for hybrid teams:

- Use activities that work for both in-person and remote participants simultaneously
- Rotate between in-person and virtual-friendly activities
- Create roles for remote participants in in-person activities (e.g., judges, timekeepers, observers)

DIY Team Building 101

"People don't need you to be perfect; they need you to be real."
—Glennon Doyle, Untamed

The biggest mistake leaders make with DIY team building is trying to replicate professional facilitation. These exercises are intended to be run between scheduled programs or before you start scheduling pro team building. It's not about polished perfection with these intermediary activities; what's important is creating opportunities for your team to experience and pursue connection.

After watching hundreds of leaders step into the facilitator role, I've learned that those who succeed show up with genuine curiosity about their team. They know everyone's name, they've learned who each person really is, and they like everyone on their team! This is what matters, not charisma, experience, or memorizing every single detail.

The following will help you move past nervousness and get started.

Build Your Activity Toolbox
Think of the activities in this book like a selection of tools. You'll need different tools for different jobs, but you don't need every tool that exists. Start with versatile basics, then expand strategically based on your team's needs.

The Core Collection
Get comfortable with foundational activities like these before adding more:

1. **Minefield**
2. **Mammoth Monument**
3. **Whadyesay?**
4. **Blindfold Maze**

The Expansion Pack

Once your core collection feels natural, expand with activities like these to serve different purposes:

5. **Bannuka**
6. **Nuclear Reactor**
7. **Frog Pond**
8. **Knot Fun**
9. **Scarecrow**

Show Up with an Attitude That Works

As you build your toolbox, approach every activity and conversation with the right attitude.

Be curious. Approach activities wondering, "What will we discover together?" instead of positioning yourself as the expert. When you're genuinely curious, you create space for organic insights rather than prescribed lessons.

Focus on the process. Emphasize "How we work together matters," not "Getting the right answer matters." The activity is just a vehicle. The real learning is how the team navigates challenges, not whether they won or completed it perfectly.

Prioritize inclusion. Communicate that "Everyone contributes something valuable," not "Some people are better at this." When you emphasize that everyone has something meaningful to offer, participation and psychological safety increase.

Follow a Progressive Skill Development Plan

If you plan to run team building activities regularly, approach facilitation as you would any other skill in life. Create a plan to build on practice, and don't pursue perfection from the start.

Here's a sample approach to help you grow your team building skills:

Month 1–2: Build Your Foundation

- **Choose 3–4 go-to activities** from our facilitators' favorites list
- **Practice** with low-stakes situations (team lunches, casual meetings)
- **Focus on logistics** so you can get comfortable with instructions and timing

Months 3–4: Expand Your Repertoire

- **Add 2–3 new activities** that work well for your team
- **Experiment with different question types** for regular connection
- **Develop timing intuition** about when to extend activities and when to wrap up
- **Practice reading the room** so you can recognize energy and engagement levels

Months 5–7: Master the Art

- **Customize 2–3 activities** to your team's specific needs and challenges
- **Start approaching resistance** and reluctance with confidence
- **Create 1–2 original variations** of standard activities

Months 8+: Ongoing Development

- **Ask for feedback** from team members about what is or isn't working
- **Talk with other leaders** who are doing similar team building efforts and learn from each other
- **Bring in professional facilitators** and pay attention to how they lead different events and activities
- **Document what works** for your team and share this when you're scheduling professional events—then, learn from how the pros respond to and implement this info

1-Month Action Plan

Theory means nothing without action. Here's a step-by-step plan to help you implement what you've learned in the first month of your larger plan:

Week 1: Choose Your First Activity

- **Select one activity from this chapter** based on what matches your team's style and your comfort level
- **Practice the instructions** until you can explain clearly without notes and say them aloud to yourself
- **Plan your timing** so you introduce the activity at a moment when people will be receptive, and you have some buffer time
- **Prepare your mindset** so you're focused on connection and celebrating mistakes, not perfection or judgment

Week 2: Try It Out

- **Introduce the activity** with some relatable context about why you're doing it
- **Pay attention to participation** and energy levels throughout the event and take notes for future activities
- **Ask for feedback** on the experience and suggestions for improvement—consider anonymous options so everyone feels safe

Week 3–4: Refine and Repeat

- **Try the same activity again** with improvements based on feedback
- **Notice what's different** the second time—you'll often see more comfort and engagement
- **Add a second activity** to your repertoire once the first feels natural
- **Start incorporating brief questions** into regular meetings

Always Adapt and Experiment

Finally, always give yourself freedom to make mistakes, iterate, and evolve. Remember:

Every team is different. What works brilliantly for one group might fall flat with another. The analytical team that loved Whadyesay? might not respond to Scarecrow the way your creative team did. That's not failure—that's valuable insights into your team's preferences.

Failure is information. This builds on the above. When activities don't work as planned, ask yourself: What didn't land? Why? What does this tell us about our team's needs or comfort level? Use this information to make better choices next time.

Every situation is unique. Adjust activities based on current energy, available time, and your goals. The same activity can serve different purposes depending on how you frame it and what you emphasize.

Evolution is expected. Your skills will grow with practice. Your team's comfort level and engagement will improve. What feels awkward in one month will feel natural in six. Trust the process!

Say Yes to Your Team

You don't need to be perfect or know exactly how your team will respond. The activities and questions in this chapter are templates and ideas that have been tested thousands of times by facilitators of all experience levels. They've all been adapted, modified, and reimagined by leaders who made them their own, and I encourage you to do the same!

Start with what feels natural. Maybe that's Frog Pond because it's fun, gets people laughing, and some of you used to play Frogger. Maybe it's Mammoth Monument because your team needs deeper connections. Maybe it's Whadyesay? because you don't feel ready for the sillier activities. All of these are valid.

We've talked a lot about embracing failure, so accept the idea that you learn something valuable when an activity doesn't land the way you hoped—you're still discovering new things about your team's preferences, comfort levels, and current needs. It's how we all learned to do this work in the first place, and it works.

You have everything you need to start *right now*:

- ◆ Proven activities that work in any environment
- ◆ Virtual and hybrid modifications for distributed teams
- ◆ Troubleshooting guidance for common challenges
- ◆ Permission to experiment and learn as you go

Trust me, your team is already waiting for more connection, whether they know it or not! They will be grateful for invitations to get to know each other better, and they'll love having opportunities to be playful and authentic.

"But David, you don't know my team," you say. You're right, I don't. But what I do know is that employees everywhere want to feel like they matter as people, not just as productivity units. I also know that there's real magic in showing up with genuine care and creating space for your staff to connect.

So, I challenge you: Say "Yes, and . . ." to this chapter! Even if it's just one activity, schedule it and *try it* in the next two weeks. Don't wait for the perfect moment—embrace vulnerability, uncertainty, and mistakes, create a plan so you can feel as ready as possible, and see what happens.

Will it be perfect? Probably not. Will you learn something valuable? Absolutely! Will your team appreciate the effort? More than you realize.

If you start small, be consistent, and stay authentic, good things happen.

Your team is ready. You're ready. The tools are here.

What will you try first?

PART IV

Making It Stick

You've seen how the best team building experiences can spark real breakthroughs—moments when people drop their guard, discover new strengths, and reconnect with a sense of purpose. But the real challenge isn't creating those moments. It's keeping them alive.

I've watched countless organizations invest in powerful experiences that spark genuine connection, vulnerability, and insight. People laugh together, discover hidden strengths, and leave feeling energized and united. Then, within weeks, it's as if nothing happened as the insights fade, old patterns return, and that carefully crafted experience becomes just another memory filed away under "fun company event."

When Results Don't Stick

I could tell you a story about this experience as I've done with Parts I, II, and III, but I'll be honest with you—this happened so many times in the early days that I wouldn't know which one to choose.

After several of these conversations, I was haunted. So I started paying attention. What was different with the teams that said the changes stuck? After investigating, taking notes, and talking to my facilitators, I figured it out: the teams that saw lasting change had more than great events—they had great debriefs and follow-through systems.

That's when I realized our job isn't just running amazing events— it's addressing sustainability so leaders know how to keep the insights alive long after everyone goes home.

We dive deep into creating sustainability in the following chapters by using powerful debriefs and integrating lessons learned into your team's day-to-day culture. These two pillars turn one-off events into long-term impact.

What You'll Discover in Part IV

1. **Chapter 10: The Debrief Is Everything**—Discover why the conversation after a team building experience often matters more than the activity itself. Learn the framework for structured reflections that turn great experiences into lasting insights.
2. **Chapter 11: From One-Off to Ongoing**—Explore ongoing practices that keep insights alive and how to integrate lessons into your team's daily operations using proven culture changes, systems, and habits. Finally, find out which metrics actually matter and how to track them.

Your Expert Guide: Rob Fletcher

I've brought in someone who's made it his life's work to support lasting changes in the teams he's worked with.

Rob Fletcher has helped more than half a million people across 200+ organizations unlock their strengths, but I picked him for Part IV because he's a master observer of human behavior. And he refuses to sugarcoat what he sees. He asks the questions that make people think and change. After decades of working with everyone from NFL teams to Giorgio Armani employees, Rob has uncovered the secrets to lasting change.

For Rob, the debrief *is* the transformation. He also brings an introvert's perspective to a field often dominated by extroverts, which helps him see the unsung heroes and quietly impactful moments. His insights come from thousands of real events, and his guidance will help you unlock sustained momentum.

His philosophy is beautifully simple: "If they don't have links to how they interact at work, it's just another cool experience that changes nothing."

Closing the Gap

This part exists to close the gap between one-offs and lasting transformation. While the activities create excitement and forge bonds, the debrief gives everything meaning. It's what helps skeptics see the value in what we do.

Think of Part IV as the bridge between inspiration and transformation. Without it, you're creating pleasant memories. With it, you're creating lasting change.

CHAPTER 10

The Debrief Is Everything

"The debrief is where the magic becomes memorable."
—Rob Fletcher

What happens *after* the activity is so important. Without reflection, even the best team building moments fade. People might laugh, connect, and solve problems together, only for the valuable insights to fade away as they return to their usual habits.

But we're not just creatures of habit, we're meaning-makers. We're wired for reflection, learning, and growth—traits that can transform an afternoon of team building into an opportunity for change. That's where the debrief comes in: it's a guided conversation that turns "That was fun!" into "That changed how we work together!"

I've mentioned how shared meals after events can spark connection, but a debrief isn't the same thing. In fact, it's better to separate the two. Dinner is where people can unwind, hang out, and start solidifying personal connections and memories. The debrief provides a structured, safe place for honest, purposeful dialogue among the whole team about the event. Both matter, but for different reasons.

A well-run debrief helps people make sense of what they learned. It bridges *fun* and *function* as teams translate experiences into insights. To shine a light on what makes that bridge hold, I asked Rob Fletcher for his thoughts on what makes the difference:

"It's about making the concepts the team building events are built around explicitly tied to their work," Rob says. "And it requires people to be vulnerable in some way—sharing something real, even something small, that helps others see them as human."

The word vulnerability has come up in every section of this book. Rob and I often reference *The Five Dysfunctions of a Team* by Patrick Lencioni, which identifies lack of trust as the first dysfunction and explains that it stems from fear of vulnerability. The irony is that the more people protect themselves from feeling vulnerable and "looking weak," the weaker their teams become.

But how much vulnerability is enough? Rob and I get that question a lot. The answer is simple. You're not asking people to share deepest secrets. You just ask questions that let them choose their own level of comfort.

For example, when running energizers, Rob suggests prompts like: "Share something that was challenging in your childhood that you're proud of overcoming."

This type of question lets everyone decide how deep or light they want to answer. One person might share about learning to ride a bike, while another might open up about overcoming a speech impediment. Both answers are valid and help form closer bonds within a team.

The good news is that, during a team building debrief, you're only seeking vulnerability and honesty in how an activity went and what people noticed, which is easier to elicit.

Ultimately, the goal is connection through honesty. And that's the foundation of every great debrief.

Turning Fun into Insight

So, how do you bridge the gap between fun and transformation?

It all comes down to asking questions that make people think about what they experienced instead of surface-level things like whether they had fun. Here's a go-to question Rob and our facilitators use:

"What did you notice about yourself or the team?"

This question shifts the focus from the activity to team dynamics. People become observers of their own behavior and that of their teammates. Instead of evaluating the activity with statements like, "Yeah, it was great," they're analyzing the experience with reflections like, "I noticed that a few of us, myself included, jumped to solutions before listening to everyone's input."

But questions alone aren't enough. Effective debriefs also require honest observations about what actually happened, and this is where Rob shines. He's never afraid to give a team his direct observations about the good, the bad, and the awkward. "I don't sugarcoat it," he explains. "I'm not mean, but I'm honest. Because they already know how they performed. They know their dynamics. What they need is someone to say it out loud so they can actually discuss it."

He learned this the hard way early in his career, watching too many facilitators fall into the trap of telling every team they're the best ever.

Honesty Pays Dividends

"Teams will ask me, 'Did we do the best of any team you've seen?'" Rob says with a laugh. "And I'll tell them, 'No, you didn't. Here's what the best looks like. But you did really well, and here's specifically where you excelled.'"

Every team—every person—wants to be the best and is afraid they're the worst. When Rob levels with them, his honesty builds trust. It shows that he's not just there to make them feel good; he's there to help them improve.

By acknowledging both the desire to be the best and the fear of failure with honesty and specificity, as Rob does, you create space for growth.

The Right Questions to Ask (and When to Ask Them)

It's essential to choose debrief questions that align with the activity, its purpose, and your team's readiness for reflection. That said, Rob has learned that you can use many of the same questions across wildly different organizations, from NFL players to Giorgio Armani executives to Sony tech teams.

"The questions can often stay remarkably similar between groups," Rob explains. "What changes is the context and examples I use to connect the concepts to their specific work."

Here's what that looks like in practice with different teams:

- **For a creative agency:** "How did the brainstorming constraints we just experienced mirror the client briefs you receive?"
- **For a tech team:** "What parallels do you see between this problem-solving challenge and debugging code?"
- **For sales teams:** "How did the communication patterns you just experienced show up in client conversations?"

Each of these questions asks how the experiences in the activity connect to actual work, but they're framed through different lenses to suit each team.

The Three-Layers Debrief Framework: From Experience to Application

"You'll often see teams from the same organization tackle the same task with completely different approaches. I love this," says Shannon. "This leads to amazing debriefs where you can ask insightful questions like, 'How did your team solve the problem?' and then ask a separate team, 'What did you all do differently to get that same end result?' That gets other teams excited to share and leads to a really natural conversation about how there are multiple ways to approach any problem. They're not right, they're not wrong, they're just different. And if they're all leading towards the same end goal, it doesn't really matter how you get there."

When you get multiple teams sharing different approaches, it highlights how many ways there are to solve one problem. The following is a simple three-layer framework you can use to run your own productive debriefs:

Layer #1: Observation—What Happened?

- What did you notice about how your team approached the challenge?
- What strategies emerged naturally?
- Where did you get stuck, and how did you get unstuck?
- What surprised you about the process?

Layer #2: Analysis—So What?

- Why do you think your team chose that approach?
- What does this tell you about how you work together?
- What patterns do you recognize from your regular work?
- What strengths became visible that you hadn't noticed before?

Layer #3: Application—Now What?

- How could you use this approach in your actual work?
- What would you do differently next time?
- What did you learn about each other that will help you collaborate better?
- What's one specific thing you'll try in your next project together?

Starting Simple: Essential Debrief Questions

If you're new to facilitating debriefs, here are some foundational questions you can ask—these work across almost any activity and are great for getting comfortable with the debrief:

- "What did you notice about yourself during that activity?"
- "What did you notice about the team?"
- "What surprised you?"
- "How might this connect to our actual work?"
- "What would you do differently next time?"

These questions work because they're aimed at the dynamics underneath the experience, encouraging self-awareness and team observation. They create space for unexpected insights and build bridges between experience and application.

As you form your own questions, remember to avoid the surface-level stuff ("How was that?" or "Did you have fun?"). These questions often produce surface-level responses or knee-jerk positive replies that lead nowhere. It's similar to how most people respond when you ask how they're doing—typically, people say they've "been good" or are doing "fine" because it's their habitual way of answering. It's just a meaningless, rote response that moves the conversation along.

If an activity was engaging and fun, watching people's energy and participation has hopefully already told you that. If it wasn't, asking won't fix it.

Does Every Activity Need a Debrief?

As important as these questions are, it's not always necessary to hold a formal debrief.

Sometimes, the most powerful reflection happens naturally when teams have space to talk among themselves after an event. Try to read the room and judge whether a debrief is necessary.

You know your team, so use your best judgment. If the energy is high and people are already processing together, it might be best if you don't force a structured conversation. Instead, create opportunities for spontaneous reflection, like extending break time or offering to order delivery so they can keep talking until lunch arrives.

The goal is insights that last, not adherence to a formula.

Going Deeper: Advanced Debrief Techniques

Once you and your team become comfortable with basic reflection and debriefs, you can introduce more advanced approaches. These techniques facilitate richer conversations that lead to deeper insights.

They highlight how the difference between adequate and exceptional debriefs often comes down to the questions you ask and how you guide teams toward meaningful connections between activities and their work.

Advanced Technique #1: Assumption-Testing Questions

These help teams examine their mental models:

- ◆ "What assumptions did you make at the start?"
- ◆ "Did those assumptions turn out to be accurate?"
- ◆ "What did you assume about your teammates that turned out to be wrong?"

These questions reveal how preconceptions shape behavior. When someone realizes they assumed a quiet colleague had nothing to contribute before they watched that person solve a critical problem, it changes how they'll interact moving forward.

Advanced Technique #2: Emotional Awareness Questions
These tap into feelings that drive behavior:

- "How did you feel when the instructions changed midway?"
- "What was your gut reaction when you hit that obstacle?"
- "Did anyone notice their stress level shifting during the activity?"

Emotions provide valuable data about team dynamics. The person who stays calm under pressure, the one who gets frustrated by ambiguity, the teammate who supports others when tension rises—these patterns show up consistently in activities and work situations.

Advanced Technique #3: Pattern-Recognition Questions
These get teams to see recurring dynamics:

- "Does this remind you of anything that happens in our normal work?"
- "Have you seen similar communication patterns in our meetings?"
- "What roles did people naturally take on? Do they play similar roles at work?"

This is where magic happens. When someone says something like, "Oh wow, this is exactly what happens when we're launching a product! We all focus on individual tasks and forget to coordinate," the debrief has done its job.

The insight doesn't come from you telling them what to notice; it comes from them making the connection.

Advanced Technique #4: The Comparison Strategy
Remember Shannon Lane DuPont from Part III? I picked this one up from her.

The Comparison Strategy gets the creative ball rolling, throws a few ideas to your team, and then lets them handle the rest. It's designed to spark conversation, and it regularly leads to brilliant discussions.

The beauty of comparison is how it can remove judgment. There's no "right" way, just different approaches with different advantages. This creates psychological safety while generating valuable insights about team dynamics.

Here's how to use this technique:

- **Highlight different approaches:** "I noticed Team A started with planning while Team B dove right into action."
- **Ask for explanation:** "Team A, what made you decide to plan first?"
- **Invite alternative perspectives:** "Did any other teams approach it differently?"
- **Draw connections:** "How do these different approaches show up in your regular work?"

The key is to present observations neutrally, invite teams to explain their reasoning, and help them recognize patterns that appear in daily collaboration.

Advanced Technique #5: The Process Focus Technique

This works well for analytical teams that enjoy deconstructing experiences and projects to learn from them. You'll know right away if it's a perfect match, and it's worth a shot if your team tends to freeze up or go into generic, checked-out responses when you ask, "How did that go?" or "What did you think of that?"

This technique focuses on specific elements of the activity and how they participated, with questions like:

- "What was the first thing your team did, and who suggested it?"
- "When did you realize you needed to change your approach?"
- "Who naturally took different roles, and how did that happen?"
- "What information did you wish you had earlier in the process?"

These questions prompt specificity. Teams can't give vague answers because you're asking about concrete moments and decisions. The resulting discussions reveal natural leadership patterns, communication styles, and decision-making approaches that impact their work.

Advanced Technique #6: The Bridge-Building Method

Explicitly connecting activity lessons to workplace situations makes it so teams don't have to make the leap on their own, and it keeps them from losing insights.

Here are some connection prompts to help you start building bridges like a master debrief engineer:

- "This reminds me of when we . . ."
- "The same thing happens in our team when . . ."
- "I wish we had this energy/approach during our . . ."
- "What if we tried this same strategy for . . ."

Start these statements yourself to model connection-making, then invite team members to complete them. Once teams see the pattern, they'll start making these connections naturally.

Pro Tip: When using the bridge-building method, be patient with silence after asking these prompts. Teams often need 10-15 seconds to make the mental connection. Resist the urge to fill the silence. That thinking time is where the learning happens.

Example Debrief: "Yes, and . . ."

Here's how a debrief might unfold after the "Yes, and . . ." improv activity from Chapter 7:

Start with Immediate Experience

- "How did it feel to be consistently agreed with?"
- "How did it feel to consistently agree with your colleagues?"
- "Was it easy or difficult to build upon what your partner said?"

Connect to Work Reality

- "Do you ever use this approach during regular work conversations?"
- "What keeps you from agreeing more often?"

Explore Applications

- "Would you appreciate it if your colleagues used the 'Yes, and . . .' approach during work meetings?"
- "Would you be willing to do the same for them?"

The progression matters. You start with the immediate experience, connect it to current reality, and then explore future possibilities. This sequence helps people process what they learned and imagine how to apply it.

When Debriefs Don't Go as Planned

Even with the best preparation and execution, debriefs sometimes hit obstacles. It happens! No one is perfect, and nothing always goes as planned. This is a normal experience, and usually indicates that the group needs more structure, clarity, or safety.

Ultimately, "advanced" facilitation isn't about control or drilling skills, but cultivating conditions where learning can happen, even in discomfort.

Let's look at common reasons a debrief can fall flat and how you can address them in the future (or on the fly) to make sure your team gets the most out of reflection time.

Issue #1: Nobody Wants to Talk

Silence doesn't always mean disengagement. Sometimes, a quiet room simply means people are still processing. The following can help you avoid this in future debriefs or pivot in the moment:

- **Start smaller:** Move to pairs or small groups before full-group discussion. People who won't speak in front of 20 colleagues often open up with two or three.

◆ **Use writing first:** Have everyone jot down thoughts before sharing. This gives introverts processing time and provides something concrete to contribute.

◆ **Share your own observations:** Model vulnerability by offering your honest reflection about what you noticed. This shows honesty is welcome and often prompts others to respond.

◆ **Lower the stakes:** Remind the group there are no wrong answers and that you're genuinely curious about their perspectives.

◆ **Change the timing:** Some teams need warm-up time before deeper sharing. If this is your first debrief, they might not be ready for depth yet. That's okay! Start surface-level and build from there.

Issue #2: One Person Dominates Every Discussion

This happens in conversations all the time—one person dominates because they're excited, eager, or more extroverted. When one voice fills the space, use structure and kindness to rebalance:

◆ **Set time limits:** Give everyone one minute to share, and enforce the limit gently but consistently.

◆ **Use equal-turn formats:** Round-robins or written input options (like virtual post-it notes) ensure everyone contributes equally.

◆ **Redirect energy:** Assign dominant speakers to leadership or summarizer roles that channel their enthusiasm productively.

◆ **Address privately:** If the pattern continues across sessions, have a private conversation. Frame it as helping the team: "I really value your insights, and I want to make sure we're creating space for other voices too. Can you help me draw out quieter team members?"

Issue #3: Conversations Stay Too Surface-Level

If discussions feel polite but shallow, add depth through curiosity, prompting, and modeling. Here are proven tactics for getting past surface-level responses and into conversations that make a difference:

◆ **Ask follow-ups:** "Tell me more about that!" or "What made you choose that approach?" These prompts signal you want deeper thinking.

- **Model depth:** Jump in first and display the level of reflection you're hoping to see. If you share something vulnerable or insightful, others often follow.
- **Connect to work:** "How does this show up in our projects?" shifts from abstract observations to concrete applications.
- **Use emotion language:** "How did it feel when . . .?" or "What was your gut reaction to . . .?" Feelings often unlock honest insights that analytical questions miss.
- **Allow silence:** Give people time to think before speaking. Comfortable silence is okay—it means people are processing. Resist the urge to fill every pause.

Issue #4: Teams Get Defensive

Defensiveness signals fear of judgment, but it can be one of the most frustrating or intimidating issues when you're new to running debriefs. Don't worry! Your job is simply to shift the focus from evaluation to learning:

- **Depersonalize feedback:** Focus on systems and strategies, not personalities. Instead of "Why didn't you communicate better?" try "What made communication challenging in that setup?"
- **Emphasize learning:** Treat outcomes as data, not verdicts on competence. "This isn't about whether you succeeded or failed—it's about what we can learn from the experience."
- **Compare approaches neutrally:** "Different teams tried different strategies" removes the hierarchy of right and wrong.
- **Highlight multiple successes:** Show there are many ways to succeed. Even unsuccessful attempts teach valuable lessons.
- **Focus forward:** "What would you try next time?" shifts attention from what went wrong to what could improve.

Issue #5: Communication Isn't Flowing

Sometimes debriefs bring underlying communication dynamics to the surface. Capitalize on these moments and turn them into lessons instead of allowing them to become disruptions.

Each person has their own way of showing up to discussions. Some dominate, others hang back, and a few wander off-topic. Rather than correcting behaviors in the moment, guide conversation and reflection through neutral observation:

- **Dominating speakers:** Invite balance. "Let's hear from some-one who hasn't spoken yet. Different perspectives help us see the full picture."
- **Quiet contributors:** Create openings. "Take a moment to jot down our thoughts before we share. It might help us find ideas we'd otherwise miss."
- **Tangent-takers:** Reground without shutting down. "That's an interesting point! Let's capture it for later and come back to our focus."

By normalizing participation variety, facilitators model respect and ensure all voices are heard.

Issue #6: Lack of Leadership Modeling

This last one is more challenging to spot—I'm including it more as a reminder than an issue you're likely to notice.

Never forget that, as the leader, you set the tone for your team before, during, *and* after games and activities. It's essential to demonstrate openness, humility, and curiosity during the debrief to show everyone that honest dialogue is safe and expected.

Here are a couple of examples:

- **Admit uncertainty:** "I may have missed something; what are you all seeing?" This gives others permission to admit uncertainty as well.
- **Address tension:** "Competition brings out different sides of all of us. What did you notice about how we work together under pressure?" Using the debrief to address any tension your team experienced during the event (especially if emotions are still high), transforms it into a positive that can build resilience and trust.

Building a Culture of Reflection

The most powerful debriefs don't happen in isolation. They're part of a broader culture where reflection becomes second nature. You can build that culture gradually by:

- **Starting small:** Try using two-minute debriefs after regular meetings. Ask, "What worked well just now?" or "What would make our next meeting more productive?" This normalizes reflection without making it feel like a big deal.
- **Building upward:** Apply similar questions to project retrospectives, after-action reviews, and major milestones. As teams get comfortable with quick reflections, they'll be ready for deeper dives.
- **Creating shared language:** Name patterns, strategies, and successes. When your team starts referring to specific approaches or insights from past activities, reflection has become part of your team's vocabulary.
- **Embedding reflection:** Include process goals in project planning, add connection questions to meeting agendas, and build collaboration metrics into performance reviews.

Over time, reflection stops being something you do at special events and becomes how your team learns and improves together. When you debrief as a fundamental way of working instead of an occasional exercise, you'll see the true power of this practice.

Adapting for Different Processing Styles

One final consideration Rob emphasized throughout our conversation is how debriefs create space for both introverted and extroverted processing styles.

Extroverts process by talking. They need opportunities to brainstorm out loud, bounce ideas off others, and think through responses in real time. Group discussions energize them.

Introverts process internally before speaking. They need time to reflect, write down thoughts, and formulate responses before sharing. Small group or one-on-one conversations work better for them.

The secret to making debriefs work for everyone isn't choosing one approach over the other. It's incorporating both. Extroversion and introversion have pros and cons, and even skilled therapists can't change someone's nature, so you need to value and work with both!

Structuring Debriefs for Your Team

Here's an approach Rob uses to honor both personality types in a single debrief:

- **Provide solo reflection time before discussion:** Even two minutes of silence can help introverts prepare and give extroverts a chance to focus.
- **Use a mix of group sizes during the debrief:** Start with pairs or trios, then move to groups of four to six, and finally bring everyone together for key insights.
- **Offer multiple ways to contribute:** Some people want time to speak, others thrive in share circles, and others still prefer writing their thoughts on a whiteboard or shared document.

As Rob puts it, "Extroverts prefer to go wide. Introverts prefer to go deep. When you design experiences that honor both preferences, everyone can connect in ways that feel natural."

The Real Power of Debriefs

The debrief is where experiences become insights. It's where "we *did this* together" transforms into "we *learned something* together." It's where laughter, challenge, and collaboration stop being just fun memories and start being catalysts for change.

The teams that skip this step or rush through it with perfunctory questions are often left with events that feel good but fade quickly, leaving no impact on how people work together. This renders team building a wasted effort and sets your business behind competitors who make the most of this tool.

Teams investing in thoughtful debriefs create a culture where reflection is valued, vulnerability is welcomed, and learning happens continuously. They don't just have better events—they become better teams.

So, start simple. Ask genuine questions, listen deeply, and create space for thinkers and talkers, for honesty and connection.

If you do this consistently, you will discover what Rob and I have both seen across thousands of events:

The debrief truly is where the magic becomes memorable.

CHAPTER 11

From One-Off to Ongoing

"Long-term impact is the biggest challenge in our industry. How do you turn a great team building experience into something that changes how people work together for years to come?"

—Rob Fletcher

In Chapter 10, we discussed the role of the debrief in long-term impact. Here, we'll take a more zoomed-out approach and look at the larger changes companies can make if they're committed to sparking lasting change.

The uncomfortable truth is that you can't ensure ongoing change with a great debrief unless your organizational practices and culture are on point. Think of it like choosing a doctor—which of these professionals would you trust your health to?

◆ **Doctor A,** who attended Harvard because they're passionate about medicine, took detailed notes and treated their education as their calling.
◆ **Doctor B,** who attended Harvard because their parents expected it, did the minimum to pass and just went through the motions to check boxes.

Both graduated from the same school, but since Doctor A was the only one truly invested in learning, they're the one that people will trust to fix their health.

The same applies to team building. If your company and its leaders show up like Dr. B—treating these events as a box to check because HR expects it—even Harvard-level facilitation won't create lasting change. It's a waste of everyone's time or risks making things worse.

I see this pattern constantly. When a client tells me team building has failed in the past, I make a note to discuss what they can do to make sure these lessons stick. Usually, the failure wasn't the activity—it was the Dr. B mentality. Fostering actual improvement and change isn't a one-time thing, and you can't phone it in. The difference in mindset makes all the difference.

Too many organizations show up like Dr. B. They treat team building as a quick fix instead of an ongoing practice. They invest in a great day, everyone has fun, and then. . . nothing. No follow-up. No reinforcement. No integration into daily work.

Even if they run a debrief, only so much can change without the right environment. This is the final piece of the sustainability puzzle.

The good news? You don't need a massive budget; you simply need to be intentional about three things:

- ◆ Creating a culture that encourages growth and connection
- ◆ Tracking and sustaining what matters
- ◆ Creating touchpoints that keep momentum alive

Remember, consistency is everything. It's like going to the gym once. You might try some exercises, feel great afterward, and maybe even benefit from the workout. But you won't see lasting results if you don't keep going back. Team building is the same—the initial experience is healthy, but you have to keep building on it to get results.

In the pages ahead, we'll revisit some crucial themes discussed throughout the book and explore how you can use everything you've learned to build systems, measure impact, shape culture, and maintain the commitment needed to go from one-off events to lasting change.

Creating a Culture of Connection

Before we explore *how* to create a culture of connection, let's be honest about why so many attempts fail. Understanding these obstacles will help you avoid them.

A big part of the problem is that many senior leaders view connection very differently from how skilled team leads view it.

"Team leaders often care deeply about bringing people together, but higher-ups tend to be too busy thinking about metrics, strategy, and the future," Rob explains. "They see progress as more important than having happy people who get along. High-level leaders are focused on guiding the ship and assume connection is HR's job."

This mindset can keep a company from reaching its goals. Even if the team leaders value connection, they can't prioritize it if higher-ups dismiss its importance. The best strategies will fail if people on all levels of the organization don't trust each other, communicate effectively, or prioritize their people.

Connection must be a strategic imperative if you want to see change, and it's everyone's job, especially upper management, to treat it as such. The first step in creating sustainability is getting leadership buy-in that team building matters as much as any other business metric.

Avoiding the Checkbox Trap

When I encounter executives who view team building as an HR requirement, my instinct is to convince them otherwise by making the business case, showing data, and explaining why connection matters. (Or, y'know, by writing a book!) But you can't argue someone into believing something. Persuasion doesn't influence people. Experience does.

These leaders have to experience it, and results speak louder than any elevator pitch or TEDTalk. When skeptical leaders participate in a well-designed event and feel the energy shift, they become believers. And when they follow through with simple actions after the event to ensure lasting change, they become fans.

No matter how hard it seems, I encourage you to give it your all, not with a half-baked event, but with a carefully crafted experience. Because if you don't, you'll risk wasted efforts.

Why Team Building Fails

When team building doesn't work, it's usually for one of three reasons.

1. Misaligned Audiences

Activities fail when they ignore individual interests and personalities. What energizes one might embarrass another. A numbers-driven finance team won't respond the same way as creatives.

Design with your audience in mind to ensure participation feels authentic, not forced.

2. Forced Participation

Nothing kills enthusiasm faster than mandatory "fun." If you pull someone from something critical, they'll disengage, and that attitude can spread fast.

Make participation voluntary when possible or schedule events with enough notice so everyone can show up ready to engage.

3. The One-and-Done Mentality

Many companies hold a single event to declare, "There, we did our team building." Then wonder why nothing changed.

Keep the momentum going, show your team building schedule, track metrics, and put daily connection practices into motion to avoid a flop.

The Expectations Problem

Another reason team building fails is unrealistic expectations. No 90-minute session can repair years of dysfunction. I've had clients call panicking about team dysfunction and say, "We had you scheduled for 90 minutes, but we're running late and need to leave early. You've got 45 minutes! I can't wait to see how this fixes things."

That's not how transformation works.

Real change takes time, clarity, and commitment. You need steady effort designed to tie experiences back into the day-to-day. Dedicate time to these changes, identify outcomes, and commit to continuing the work at the office.

If you expect miracles with minimal time investment, attention, or follow-through, you'll be disappointed.

Yes, team building improves relationships, strengths, and interdependence. But to experience these benefits, it has to be part of your culture and mindset, not an isolated event. And culture starts at the top. If leadership treats connection as optional, your team will too.

Getting Leadership Buy-In

Before you assume this doesn't apply to your company, consider this: As of 2024, Gallup's *State of the Global Workplace* found that only 20% of employees strongly agree they feel connected to their organization's culture.[1] That means roughly 80% of workers are showing up without the engagement and emotional investment that drive innovation and collaboration! These people are doing their jobs, but they're not building anything together or creating the kind of magic that separates good companies from exceptional ones.

I talked about this a lot in Chapters 2 and 4—if you think this may be an issue that holds you back, I encourage you to revisit these chapters and make a plan to change.

The Three Pillars of Lasting Connection

When team building succeeds, it's because organizations get specific about what they're trying to improve. Design experiences and imperatives that address your goals, commit to sustained effort to achieve them, and turn every lesson along the way into something impactful. Your team needs time for the experience and the debrief, they need you to reinforce what was learned so they can do it again, and they need a structure that fosters the changes you want to see.

It's a continuous cycle of building on and addressing their needs until those needs are met.

Through thousands of conversations with facilitators and leaders, and years of watching what makes changes stick, I've found three core practices that turn short-term team building into long-term connection. You've probably even begun to identify these yourself while reading the book—they're *that* essential.

The following should each be something your company culture fosters:

Pillar #1: Get to Know Each Other as Humans

The first pillar is about the biggest theme of this book: connection.

"You have to get to know each other as people first," Rob emphasizes. "You should know each other as well as possible. Ask questions like, 'How can I view this person three-dimensionally instead of just a name on an email signature?'"

This is simple but revolutionary. Most workplaces treat people as functions. You might know Sarah as "the project manager" or James as "the guy in finance," but who are they beyond that?

When team members see each other as real people, it becomes easier to navigate conflicts, collaborate, and show empathy. Team building creates structured opportunities for people to show up as themselves and share pieces of their lives so everyone can build these invaluable three-dimensional views of each other.

Pillar #2: Adopt a Strengths-Based Focus

This second pillar is about embracing equity while dispelling the idea that everyone can and should do everything equally well.

"We all have peaks and valleys," Rob says. "It's inaccurate to believe that everybody can do the same job equally well. Good strengths-based teams are built from specialists—creative thinkers, marketing pros, project managers, relationship builders, analytical problem solvers, and detail-focused operators."

It's important to recognize and celebrate what each person does best instead of fitting everyone into the same mold. Encourage people to lean into their strengths and rely on teammates to handle what they struggle with. When you do this, three amazing things happen:

- **Quality improves** because people operate in their genius as opposed to grinding through their weaknesses.
- **Appreciation deepens** because people recognize their teammates' value in areas where they struggle.
- **Psychological safety increases** because people enjoy being valued for what they do best instead of worrying about having their weaknesses exposed.

Understanding your team's preferences and communication styles is essential. It tells you how they work best, what energizes them, and where their strengths lie, so you can stop trying to change them and start creating conditions where they can thrive.

Pillar #3: Maximize Face-To-Face Time for Connection

This third pillar is all about using your face-to-face time wisely.

This isn't just for remote and hybrid teams—while it's true that today's teams are often divided across the country or world, this pillar is important for every company, which is why I said "face-to-face time," not "in-person time."

If your team is hybrid or remote, this section refers to the rare times when you get everyone together. If your whole team works on-site, "face-to-face time" refers to those moments when everyone is away from their desks.

"When remote and hybrid teams have invaluable in-person time, really focus on interactive experiences instead of work," Rob advises. "You get groups that want to fly everybody over from different continents to spend three days 'connecting.' Then they end up locking everyone in a dark room for that time to make them watch a PowerPoint. They could've done that at home. It's a terrible use of in-person time."

If you invest in bringing people together physically, or if you take a day away from your desks, don't waste it on meetings and presentations. Prioritize face-to-face for the things that truly benefit from being present together: reading body language, building rapport, having fun, solving problems in real time, and connection experiences that create shared memories and inside jokes.

"It's tough when you're working with teams hired in 2020 or later, where people have collaborated for years but never met in person," Rob says, laughing. "So much of what we get is from body language and expressions. Then they spend that time on PowerPoints instead of connecting."

Finally, for the teams that will never meet in person, remember that virtual connection can work beautifully when done thoughtfully. The right events can make a world of separation feel like nothing.

My point is, no matter how your team works, value the moments you have to reconnect, reflect, and remember why you're doing this work together, and don't muddle them with work or boring presentations.

Beyond the Pillars: Practical Daily Connection

The three pillars provide the foundation, but connection only lasts when it's woven into daily routines. These five high-impact habits can help make connection part of how your team works:

1. Recognize and Appreciate Each Other

Make appreciation specific. Don't just say "good job"—say why it mattered. Recognition fuels connection because people feel seen and valued for their strengths.

> **Pro Tip:** Recognition isn't one-size-fits-all. Some people love public shout-outs, others prefer private acknowledgment. Use the Employee Recognition Survey in the appendix to learn different ways to show appreciation.

2. Be Curious

As Rob says, "Curiosity is a long-lost art that literally makes you smarter. Certainty just makes you kind of smart." Great things happen when you ask genuine questions. Ask teammates what excites them, what's been challenging, or what they're learning lately. This creates connections faster than almost anything else.

3. Lead by Example

Your behavior sets the tone. When you're open, authentic, and curious, your team follows. Model what you want to see: admit when you don't know things, celebrate others' wins, and share credit freely. When leaders lead like humans, teams respond in kind.

4. Build Reflection into Regular Workflows

Don't save reflection for quarterly reviews. Add five-minute check-ins after meetings and apply the lessons from Chapter 10. The more natural the reflection becomes, the more your team learns and connects.

5. Create a Team Language

Give the patterns, strategies, and successes you observe unique names. When something works well, call it out and label it so you can reference it later. Creating shortcuts and insider lingo encourages communication and shared identity.

Consistency Makes This Sustainable

These pillars and connection strategies only work with consistency. Remember how many companies I've talked to that wondered why nothing changed after an event? This is a huge part of how you avoid that trap. You can't create connections with a single team building event any more than you can build fitness with a single workout. The goal is to integrate connection with how your team operates. It's not a program with a start and end—it's a mindset.

Start small. Pick two or three connection strategies from above and apply them daily for a month. Hold yourself accountable with a checklist. At the end of the month, consider what changed, ask for feedback, then add another. Over time, these habits come naturally, and that's when you know you've built a genuinely connected culture.

Then, start changing your company culture to reflect the three pillars. Get buy-in on every level. Make sure real changes are happening consistently.

Tracking Change: KPIs That Actually Matter

Business leaders love their metrics—dashboards with numbers, percentages, and trend lines are tailor-made to make people feel confident they understand what's happening. But measuring connection and team effectiveness is trickier than tracking quarterly revenue.

The most important things are often hard to quantify. You can't put "team trust" and "psychological safety" into a spreadsheet and watch them turn green when you hit targets. But you can't ignore these metrics. You need to choose the right ones and do something with the data you collect.

The Assessments Worth Using

If you're going to use formal assessments, two consistently provide valuable insights into team building:

The Five Dysfunctions of a Team Assessment

Patrick Lencioni's framework tracks five vital areas—trust, conflict, commitment, accountability, and results. Run it before your team building initiative and again every six months as you keep applying what you're learning. It'll show whether you're moving the needle on the fundamentals that make teams work.

Gallup's Q12 Engagement Survey
Gallup's 12-question survey measures engagement, belonging, and performance. It asks questions that surprise leaders, like "Do I have a best friend at work?"

I've seen executives roll their eyes at this, but these questions were chosen because they're strong predictors of engagement and retention. Collect baseline data before you focus on connection and team building, and again every six months.

Observational Metrics Worth Tracking
These formal assessments are valuable, but the most revealing metrics are often the ones you see and feel every day:

- **Energy and tone:** Is there laughter and ease, or tension and silence?
- **Collaboration:** Do people readily reach out for help, or work in silos?
- **Turnover:** Are you losing your best people, or do they stay and bring others with them?
- **Conflict:** Are disagreements resolved constructively, or avoided entirely?

The trick to measuring these patterns is to answer honestly. You can track them based on your own observations or turn them into a regular survey for everyone or team leaders.

Metrics That Waste Everyone's Time
Not all measurements are useful. The worst are one-and-done surveys you never speak of again. Organizations will spend big money on 360 reviews or "team temperature" reports that vanish into an untouched shared drive.

This is a waste of time and damages your reputation with your team. If you're not prepared to act on what you learn, don't do it. Empty promises tell your team, "We don't care what you think, we're just checking boxes."

When we ran DISC training with our own team years ago, we turned it into action. Everyone posted notes on their doors about how to best communicate with them, and in days, people were engaging differently. *That's* what good measurement does: it changes behavior in small but meaningful ways.

These habits can help you track metrics effectively without creating busywork:

◆ **Start with 2–4 metrics:** Don't track everything. Pick measures that align with your challenges and goals.

◆ **Plan your follow-through first:** Before collecting data, decide how you'll share results, what actions you'll take, and who's responsible.

◆ **Mix numbers with stories:** Use assessments and observations. Numbers tell you something happened; stories tell you what it means.

◆ **Measure consistently:** Baseline + regular follow-ups = progress tracking.

◆ **Be transparent:** Share what you're measuring and why. Involve the team in solutions.

◆ **Accept what you can't quantify:** The absence of measurable data doesn't mean nothing's happening. Some changes—like shifts from suspicion to trust, or isolation to connection—show up in subtle ways that defy quantification.

The goal isn't proving team building works. It's noticing whether your efforts are creating the changes your team needs. Stay curious, stay observant, and act on what you learn.

Building a Practice, Not Just an Event

The shift from one-off events to lasting impact isn't complicated. It requires commitment from a leadership that views connection as strategic, systems that integrate reflection, and abandoning the illusion that a single day can transform how people work long-term.

Nobody gets in shape from one workout, learns a language from one lesson, or builds a strong relationship from one conversation. The same is true for team building. The initial experience plants ideas, creates openings, and establishes new patterns of interaction, but you have to keep practicing if you want it to change how your team operates day to day.

Approach follow-through with passion and avoid checking team building off your list—that's how transformation happens. The leaders who pull this off weave the lessons their team learns into the fabric of their organization's operations.

The activities matter. The debriefs matter. But what matters most is the weekly check-ins, acknowledgments in meetings, and the intentional moments of connection that remind people why they're working together. It's the leader who references "remember when we built that pipeline together?" during a difficult project. It's the team that applies lessons from a communication exercise when tension rises. It's the organization that treats connection as essential to performance, not separate from it.

So before you plan your next team building event, ask yourself: Am I doing this to check a box, or am I building a system? Am I creating an isolated experience, or designing something that integrates into how we work? Am I hoping for magic in an unrealistic timeframe, or committing to the ongoing work transformation requires?

The answers to those questions will determine whether your efforts create lasting impact or fade into another pleasant memory. If you're serious about building teams that collaborate, communicate, and support each other through challenges, then you have to be serious about sustainability.

Team building isn't just an event, it's a practice. The difference between the two is temporary inspiration vs. lasting change. And that difference shows up in every metric that matters, from retention to innovation to results.

Conclusion: The Future of Teams Is Human

We've explored the science, strategy, and soul of team building as I've come to know it. Together, we've covered topics ranging from neuroscience to DIY games to the secrets behind why some events fall flat while others create lasting memories.

My efforts in this industry have always been about helping people share laughter, vulnerability, and trust with their peers and move beyond job titles and Slack handles.

Each section, each chapter, has been building toward this one truth:

The future of teams depends on extraordinary leaders willing to invest in the human need to find connection, purpose, and belonging. In this sense, the future of teams depends on team building.

How This Book Came to Be

Initially, I thought this book would be a straightforward founder's story, from basement murder mystery dinners to working with companies like Apple and Google. But as I talked about it, I realized that this wasn't just my story.

This book needed to be about people. It needed to focus on how connection changes lives, how purpose builds culture, and how family—both literal and workplace—shapes everything we do.

So, I changed my approach. This wouldn't be me sitting alone writing about myself. I wanted to find others to contribute, in honor of the connection that has shaped my work, so we could tell this story together. I made this book a blueprint for what's possible when leaders invest in their teams with intentionality.

The Voices That Shaped This Journey

You've heard from some of the most incredibly insightful facilitators and team building experts I know: Julia Holladay, Tyler Hayden, Paul Giroux, Shannon Lane DuPont, Jayne Hannah, and Rob Fletcher. Each brought their insights, making this book what it is. I couldn't have done it without them.

In this last chapter, I'm bringing in four more experts: my wife, Wendy; my daughters, Sam and Baylee; and my son, Ty. They've all been integral to TeamBonding's success, the creation of this book, and my sanity through all of it:

- **Wendy** is our Operations Manager and the behind-the-scenes magic here. She's the glue holding everything together, bringing much-needed creativity, fun, and energy to the office and to every event we create. She often adds the little extra touches in the background that make our events unforgettable.

- **Sam** is our Director of Sales and the connector, always in tune with our clients' needs and the pulse of the industry. She brings big-picture thinking with an eye for meaningful details, guiding teams, clients, and partners toward memorable experiences that feel both thoughtful and effortless. Her energy is conta-  gious, her creativity is boundless, and she turns vision into reality.

- **Baylee** is our Creative Director and our master of strategy, event planning, and business development. She brings passion to everything she touches and has an uncanny ability to find the threads that help people connect and have fun.

- **Ty** brings an outside perspective from his work in operations at a major corporation. While he's not part of TeamBonding's day-to-day, his insights into what today's teams need—flexibility, connection, meaningful work—ground this book in the reality in which employees are living.

Why Team Building Matters More Than Ever

"Connection isn't just nice—it's what starts progress."
—Baylee Goldstein

In 2025, we're seeing a massive shift in how we work. Remote teams. Distributed cultures. Generational turnover. Automation. AI. Economic headwinds. Quiet quitting. Burnout. Pick your buzzword—it's a lot.

Baylee's perspective on this comes from the frontlines as our Creative Director. "Team building creates a rare chance to be seen by leadership beyond your daily tasks," she told me. "It's one of those few spaces where people can showcase who they really are through creativity, leadership, potential, personality . . . We have AI actively reshaping jobs right now, so it's those human qualities that set people apart. These spaces created by team building are also where people get noticed. It's where they find new opportunities and even promotions."

We do live in a very different world from the one in which I founded TeamBonding. When employees get to express these parts of themselves—their creativity and personality—alongside their leaders, they're not seen for what they do, but for *who they are*. That visibility opens doors for connection, advancement, and trust.

So many employees go months or years without ever being seen as more than a literal human resource. When you add team building to the mix, you create a beautiful pause in this often inescapable pattern that allows people to show up as real individuals, not just job functions. As Baylee reminded me, this matters even more in a hybrid or remote world where connection doesn't always happen naturally.

Sam has also witnessed this shift from her role working with TeamBonding's clients. "Team building is essential because there are fewer organic connections in the office now, fewer casual interactions as you're walking by someone," she says. "There's a risk of silos and miscommunications when you're Slack-ing or messaging rather than being in person. Team building solves that by intentionally recreating connection and collaboration between people when they come together, even if they're remote or hybrid."

She also highlighted the generational gaps in today's workplaces and the importance of bridging them through shared experiences. There are indeed five generations in today's workforce, and many younger workers are starting out remote. They're not learning by watching office interactions or hearing what executives say at the water cooler. So how do they make those connections? How do they learn? Team building is a good start. It helps create the bonding and shared experiences that used to happen naturally.

"A lot of jobs work from home. For me, I see my team and my teammates probably once a quarter, maybe a couple here and there every month or so," Ty adds. "It can be a very isolating experience, especially when you work for a larger company or corporation." He went on to express how team building has given him crucial breaks from what he calls the "monotonous feeling of having to do the same task" and how it helps everyone "understand the people behind the employees you work with."

The Power of Purpose

> *"When people serve together, they connect on a deeper level.*
> *It's not just camaraderie, you're part of something bigger."*
>   —Sam Goldstein

Today's workforce considers culture, values, and a sense of purpose when choosing jobs. When employees build bikes for kids or assemble care packages for underserved families, they're seeing that the company they work for is about more than just profits, and they know they chose well. Time and time again, I hear participants tell me how proud they are that their company cares about people and communities.

Wendy sees this from the operations and people side, saying, "Humans need interaction. We need to know that we're there for each other, that we can trust each other, that we can depend on each other on a personal and professional level."

Wendy has watched how our own team—some in the office full-time, some hybrid, others remote—has responded to the days we schedule in-house team building. "Those are the days that remind them that they're not in an isolated world and that they're part of a larger community. Bringing our team together encourages communication, shows support, and definitely improves the overall morale at our company," she says.

Baylee pointed out another powerful aspect of the purpose we help create: *upskilling through impact*. She loves seeing how it helps people build new skills, connect to a greater purpose, and bond with each other at the same time. It's not every day you get a chance to do something like that.

"Companies have the opportunity to offer volunteer experiences that don't just do good, but also build relevant skills for their employees and help everyone connect," she said. "If you're mentoring students or teaching digital literacy or supporting STEM programs, you're not just benefiting the community—you're also developing leadership, communication, and adaptability within your team."

Ty has also witnessed this transformation through CSR events: "I think that giving back kind of opens you to a new avenue of the people you work with—how they act, their motivations, what drives them, and why they want to serve the community. And when employees see that their company's willing to put in money, time, effort so they can give back, whether it's big or small, whether it's time or money, I think it opens their eyes."

The True Meaning of Belonging

This is a theme that came up a lot when I talked about this book with my family, and my favorite part was how Baylee challenged me to think about what belonging really means in the workplace:

> "I think belonging means something different than how it's often interpreted," Baylee explains. "It means that you belong as a unique individual within a group—you're valued because you're a wonderfully complex person who brings something different. We all want to feel safe and connected. When we truly come together as a team to combine our different strengths from a place of acceptance, we're able to innovate more because our differences aren't just accepted but celebrated."

What Baylee's getting at is crucial: diversity is about who's in the room, but belonging is about whether those people feel welcome and safe enough to be themselves. When you have diverse voices in the room AND those people feel they truly belong, you'll have healthy disagreement, fresh perspectives, and innovation. You need people who contradict each other, voice conflicting ideas, and make connections based on their unique life experiences.

"I always think about how men were the only ones designing tampons for decades—for decades, women weren't in the room—and I wonder how different that would have been if their perspective were included," Baylee adds. "Or how advancements in STEM are happening now because there are different genders and backgrounds and voices finally working together. True innovation comes from connection, from people bringing the differences they live into spaces where they feel that sense of belonging."

Belonging is the foundation that enables you to stand out and embrace your unique viewpoint with confidence. Teams aren't stronger when everyone is the same; they're stronger when you have a mix of voices, perspectives, and strengths from each person in a group that understands inclusion and belonging. I hope to contribute to this by designing experiences where people feel safe enough to show up as their whole, authentic selves and have those differences be valued, not smoothed over.

The Family Factor

There's nothing quite like knowing that I built this company along-side my family—if you want to talk about belonging, this is *it* for me. I see the people closest to me bringing new perspectives to the table, which helps me to appreciate them in all these new ways. And when I get to watch my family help others connect, I end up wanting to help teams everywhere experience similar joy.

Instead of explaining this in my words, though, I want you to hear it from theirs:

> "I think it's incredible, and I feel so fortunate that I've gotten to see my children grow and thrive in their positions at work. I've seen them as leaders. I've watched them manage teams. It's such a gift, and not a day goes by that I don't feel fortunate to have been given this opportunity that not many parents get! At work, I don't feel like they're my children. I see them as incredibly capable coworkers. Working side by side with David, we don't know any other way. We've always worked and lived together, and our family naturally grew around that. We all live and breathe TeamBonding in our dinner conversations, in the car, and on walks. It's our life."
>
> —Wendy Goldstein

> "When we work as a family, we have this automatic trust and loyalty, and there's nothing better than that. If you knew that every single one of your employees was going to be loyal

forever and connected to you, that's what it's like. And there's this luckiness and gratitude that comes with it. It makes work feel personal, which I think is actually a good thing. Even when we disagree, we're all on the same team, and that's just so incredible. So I always ask myself, how can we recreate something similar for other teams? If we're so lucky that we have this loyalty built in, how do you build loyalty on other teams? It's such an important experience to me that I want to help others benefit from something similar."

—Sam Goldstein

"Working with family taught me that you can disagree, push each other, and still come out stronger. There's nothing wrong with some friction because underneath it all, there's a lot of trust, and that's what makes it work. Your family knows your strengths and habits, so they can hold you more accountable in ways that make you better. That's what every team needs— the safety to challenge each other, knowing the foundation of trust won't break. You also need safety to mess up sometimes and know that no one will think less of you."

—Baylee Goldstein

"Growing up, dinner conversations were always about work problems and solutions, and I watched TeamBonding evolve from our basement to what it is today. It was unbelievable and motivating to see—this is what happens when you work hard and don't give up. The biggest thing was the passion. That's what mattered—making sure this is successful, making sure people are taken care of, and making sure these events go well. And the coolest thing you guys do is the service side, whether it's the bike builds or whatever it is nowadays. That part will never go out of fashion. That's what you should be most proud of because the actual event is affecting the community."

—Ty Goldstein

This experience is what we're trying to build everywhere. Not literal family businesses, but teams that operate with that same level of trust, loyalty, and genuine care for one another as we all enjoy. We've all dedicated ourselves to this mission, and I'm so honored to work alongside my beautiful family as they help me bring this joy to the lives of thousands every single year.

What's Really at Stake

"People need to connect. They need to communicate. They need empathy and gratitude."

—Wendy Goldstein

I've seen what happens when organizations don't prioritize human connection—it puts everything on the line, and they often don't even realize it.

"Ultimately, your business is at stake," agrees Sam. "We're talking about your people, your performance, and your reputation as an employer. If there's no real human connection, people won't stay or believe in what you're building. In a fast-paced, high-pressure environment, if you're not making space for people to feel valued, supported, and to have a little fun, stress rises, morale drops, and turnover follows. Human connection isn't a 'nice to have,' it's the difference between a team that thrives and a team that burns out."

When your people don't feel valued, they're not going to rave about where they work because it's just another job. But when connection and belonging are built into your culture? Those employees become your greatest ambassadors. They're the ones posting about your company, telling their networks how amazing it is to work there, and coming to work genuinely happy. That's the kind of culture that attracts and retains the best people.

"And when people feel that way, it doesn't just create a nice vibe, it drives the business," adds Sam. "Happy, connected employees perform better, sell better, collaborate better, and bring in new customers through positive reputation alone. When you invest in belonging and human connection, people carry that energy into every conversation they have, inside and outside the organization. That's how culture becomes your competitive advantage."

Wendy put a capstone on this topic, saying, "At the end of the day, everyone needs to connect. We're human, so we need to communicate. We need to feel empathy and gratitude, and we need to know that we're appreciated. When business owners and leaders realize how much their people matter, and they build everything around it, they're suddenly leaps and bounds ahead of everyone else. It happens because they stop looking outward and build a solid foundation from within. That's where the magic is."

These truths are worth repeating because they're fundamental to everything we've discussed. I find it tragic when businesses overlook the human element, and so beautiful when you see those thriving companies that obviously get it. The more leaders who step up and start looking at things differently, the better.

A Challenge to Every Leader

"If you're not growing and developing your people, are you really respecting them?"

—Ty Goldstein

If I could have a conversation with every leader who ever reads this book, I'd offer this challenge: Think of your people differently. Stop thinking of them as resources and start seeing them as the reason your company exists.

I'm aware that this sounds simple, even obvious, but I've spoken with hundreds of leaders, and so many will say that they value their people while their actions tell a completely different story. They have to be honest with themselves about how their people actually feel and be willing to invest in things that don't show immediate ROI. That's what this challenge is really asking of you.

"Exactly. People are not resources—resources are meant to be used and replaced," adds Baylee. "People are invaluable parts of your company, meant to be invested in, inspired, and supported so they can grow. The leaders who measure success by short-term finances alone are losing long-term sustainability. The companies that thrive in the long run will always prioritize their people. They're the companies out there measuring success in loyalty, retention, and innovation instead of just looking at revenue."

"I think a lot of the problem is this trickle-down effect where leaders tell their team what needs to be done because of their deadlines," comments Ty. "They're just thinking about what needs to be completed. But there are different ways of going about it that can help employees feel more valued and get more enjoyment from what they're doing, and that improves productivity, so everyone wins."

He also identifies a critical disconnect: "What leadership thinks they need is a good salary and good benefits, which of course is important, but I think what employees are looking for is that flexibility and the power and control of their own job. People lose interest in their job when they feel like they're just doing the work for somebody else."

This disconnect is everywhere. Leaders think the problem is compensation or that their employees are mad about not having this benefit or that, but they're really looking for purpose and autonomy. They don't want to feel like cogs in a machine, and that's exactly *why* this challenge matters so much.

"To me, this challenge is about remembering that your team is made of real humans, not just roles or resources," says Sam. "When leaders only look at the numbers—revenue, output, efficiency—they end up missing the deeper story. The real drivers of performance are the relationships inside your organization, the sense of purpose your people feel, and their day-to-day well-being.

"When people feel supported, valued, and genuinely connected, they show up differently: more creative, more loyal, more energized," she continues. "And yes, the numbers follow. Focusing on people first isn't 'nice-to-have' culture work; it's the strategy that makes everything else possible. You wouldn't have a company without your people. So care for them, invest in them, and watch what happens when they thrive."

This isn't just philosophy for us—Wendy has been living and meeting this challenge every day. As the lifeblood of TeamBonding's team, she puts so much of her heart into being there for the people within this company.

"Leaders would benefit so much from accepting a challenge to focus more on their people's potential rather than just results or numbers," she tells me. "Instead of only caring about tasks and outcomes, leaders should aim to build trust, give people purpose, and allow them freedom to grow. I would challenge them to support and develop people by caring and recognizing their potential."

She went on to add to this from her operational perspective: "We work really hard to create a workplace where employees feel valued and respected, which leads to higher engagement, productivity, and loyalty. There's nothing like walking into our events room and hearing everyone laughing and joking. That's a morale booster right there."

Years ago, Wendy and I didn't realize how much we needed to emphasize our employees' happiness and well-being. Yes, we cared about our people, but work was still just work. You came in, completed your tasks, and stayed well over your scheduled hours. We definitely got some things wrong in those days, if I'm being honest, because we thought that providing fair treatment and steady work was enough. And maybe it was at the time, but as the world changed, we realized it wasn't enough anymore. So, we learned. We evolved.

Wendy reflected on this, "Now we put so much emphasis on employee well-being. These days, we really pay attention, we listen, we care, and we make sure everyone has a healthy work-life balance. We also make sure everyone has a good salary and company perks! We do food truck Tuesdays, we have a summer Friday schedule, and we even have a wellness app! And, of course, we facilitate ongoing team building programs to practice what we preach. I'm also proud to say that we reevaluate our company benefits every year to stay up to date and offer our employees the most that we can."

Wendy was a driving force behind our efforts to keep up with the times, embrace generational diversity, and learn what *people* need to thrive. She's helped us foster a good attitude and a workplace people actually enjoy.

This evolution didn't happen overnight, and we're not done yet. No business should ever quit evolving! We'll step up to meet every new challenge, every new expectation, and each new opportunity to show up better for our team. This challenge isn't just for others—it's one I hold myself to every single day.

Keep Playing. Keep Building. Keep Belonging. Keep Giving

"It's all about staying curious and human. No matter how much the workplace changes, playing sparks creativity and breaks down barriers."

—Baylee Goldstein

Leaders who accept this challenge will inevitably ask: "Okay, but what does this actually look like? What are the practices that make this real?"

I've spent decades building TeamBonding around a few core principles that have never failed us. These aren't tactics that have changed with the latest business trends; they're fundamental human needs that will matter as much in 10 years as they do today.

Keep Playing

Play is the secret to driving creativity and lowering the walls between us. Never forget that play is where innovation begins. It's where trust is built, where people remember they're human *beings*, not just human "doings."

Keep Building

We're not just building companies, but communities. Not just teams, but movements. Not just events, but ecosystems of connection that sustain people through the hard times and amplify the good times.

Keep Belonging

By creating spaces where differences are celebrated, we can continue to foster this sense of belonging. It's about making sure work is a place where authenticity is rewarded, where people can show up as their whole selves and be valued for exactly who they are.

Keep Giving

When teams engage together and give, they're using their time and skills for something they care about, and that unlocks a deeper layer of connection. This is where people feel proud of where they work and genuinely connected to their teammates in ways that ordinary projects simply can't replicate.

So let's keep playing. Keep building. Keep belonging. Keep giving. Keep listening. Keep learning. Keep showing up for each other with empathy, gratitude, and the recognition that we're all in this together.

The Legacy That Lives in People

"Legacy is not leaving something for people. It's leaving something in people."
—Peter Strople, speaker and leadership expert

No matter how passionate I am about team building, I don't want myself or TeamBonding to be remembered for the events we ran or the brands we served, but for how we made people feel.

Instead, I'd like to know that, every day, someone walks into work and feels just a little more seen, heard, and connected because of something we sparked. I'd like for the companies we work with to realize and appreciate that their greatest asset isn't their product or profits, but their people.

Ultimately, I'd like to impact this world with moments instead of monuments, stories instead of structures, and transformations instead of transactions.

These are the things that live in people long after we're gone.

TeamBonding isn't just my story, though—it's my family's story as well. So I asked Wendy, Sam, Baylee, and Ty what legacy means to them:

"I want to be part of creating unforgettable experiences. The most meaningful moments for me are when clients come back and say, 'We're still talking about the bike build we did five years ago.' That's so cool to me that we're able to bring people together to have fun, laugh, give back, and then want to do it again. I sort of live to hear people say things like, 'I worked with this company 10 years ago and we did a bike build with you. Now I'm at a new company and we want to do something similar because it was so awesome.' So that's the legacy I want us to leave—unforgettable joy."

—Sam Goldstein

"For me, the legacy I want to leave is simple. I want work to feel more human. I want people to walk into work and feel like it's a warmer place, where you don't have to sit next to someone for years without knowing who they really are. Instead, you can learn that your colleague has kids or that you share a passion for cooking or similar struggles. Those little moments of connection change everything. They make work feel less transactional and more meaningful. Connection is what pushes the world forward. Sometimes it's just about being in the right space at the right time."

—Baylee Goldstein

"I'd hope to leave a legacy where we helped people feel good about themselves, you know? I want them to feel good about the work they're doing and the difference they've made in others' lives. I'm honored that we get to be a part of that."

—Wendy Goldstein

Now It's Your Turn

The future of teams isn't about technology, tactics, or trendy frameworks.

It's about trust.

It's about seeing each other.

It's about creating conditions where people can do their best work *and* be their best selves.

Real people are behind every successful project, product, and company. These people crave experiences, connection, purpose, and the chance to matter.

With this in mind, I remind you: The future of work is human. And the best part? We get to create it.

Every team building event, conversation, and intentional moment of connection represents a brick in the foundation of a more human workplace and world. Trust me, your team is ready, your people are waiting, and the tools you need are in your hands.

So now it's your turn . . .

To build something beautiful.

To create a legacy that lives in people, not just in profit margins.

To prove that when companies truly invest in their people—with action instead of words—everything else follows.

It all starts with *you.*

So, thank you for reading. Thank you for caring. Thank you for being part of this movement toward more human workplaces.

Now, go make something amazing happen!

—David Goldstein

Founder of TeamBonding

Appendix: Employee Recognition Survey

Use this survey to understand how each team member prefers to be recognized for their contributions. Recognition that aligns with personal preferences creates more meaningful impact than one-size-fits-all approaches.

How I Like to Be Recognized

Select all that apply:

- Give me more feedback
- A simple "Thank You"
- Let me work on projects that excite and challenge me
- Allow me time during the work week to work on a charity project that's important to me
- Give me opportunities to grow professionally and move up in the company
- Give me a gift card for: _____
- Help fund my continuing education
- Pay for my training courses
- Give me a symbolic trophy or reward
- Help me stay fit and healthy (pay for my gym/wellness membership)
- Give me extra PTO
- Recognize my lifestyle (Allow me the flexibility to leave my desk during the day to walk my dog, or take time off during the week to take a course)
- Go out to celebrate
- Other: _____

When I Like to Be Recognized

Select one or more:

- Surprise me
- As soon as I hit achievements
- During a review that is:
  - Quarterly
  - Semi-annually
  - Annually
  - Other: _____
- Other: _____

How I Like to Receive Recognition

Select your preference:

Make It Public! Let Everyone Know Via

- Social media
- Internal messaging (e.g., Slack or intranet)
- Kudos board
- Company newsletter
- Company website

Keep It Private

- I'd appreciate a private message or a handwritten note
- Keep it private with an email, but feel free to loop in senior leaders in the company

Using This Survey: Best Practices

1. **Administer during onboarding** or annual reviews so preferences are documented from the start
2. **Store responses confidentially** and share only with managers who need to know
3. **Revisit annually** as preferences change over time and with life circumstances

4. **Honor the preferences**—public recognition for someone who requested privacy can backfire
5. **Use as a conversation starter** about what makes team members feel valued

Remember, recognition is most powerful when it's:
- Specific (tied to actual achievements)
- Timely (close to when the contribution happened)
- Sincere (genuinely felt and expressed)
- Personalized (aligned with how the person wants to be recognized)

Additional Energizers

Rock-Paper-Scissors Showdown
Time: 5–10 minutes | **Group Size:** 10–100+ | **Materials:** None

This isn't your childhood rock-paper-scissors. It's a high-energy tournament that transforms a simple game into a hilarious group experience; it's guaranteed fun that breaks down walls faster than I could have imagined.

I've watched interns and CEOs cheering side-by-side within the first two minutes. A lot of events spend the first 10 minutes just figuring out what they're doing, so this sort of instant result is incredibly valuable.

Deploy this when you need to transition from low energy to high energy *fast*.

How to Play

1. Everyone pairs up for a single round of rock-paper-scissors
2. Those who lose take on the role of enthusiastic cheerleaders for the winners
3. Winners face winners; losers join the growing cheering squads
4. Continue until a final champion emerges with an army of supporters

Why We Love It

- **Instant energy boost:** Gets everyone moving and laughing immediately
- **Eliminates self-consciousness:** Everyone's being silly together
- **Natural team building:** Cheering squads create spontaneous collaboration
- **Scales infinitely:** Works with 10 people or 1000
- **No setup required:** Can be deployed instantly when energy flags

---

Virtual Adaptation: This translates surprisingly well to video calls! Use gallery view and ask everyone to exaggerate their movements to be more visible.

Gotcha

Time: 5 minutes | **Group Size:** 10–50 | **Materials:** None

This one's sneaky brilliant. It looks simple, and it is, but it sparks instant laughter and a kind of shared mischief that creates fast bonds. It's a reflexes and focus game that creates laughter and friendly competition, and it's worth trying at least once to see if it clicks with your team.

The beauty of this is that everyone fails together in the first round, and that shared laugh creates more bonding than 30 minutes of forced small talk ever will.

"This one requires touching," Shannon warns, "so you do want to make sure your team and environment are appropriate for physical interaction ahead of time!"

How to Play

- Participants form a circle
- Each person places their left hand out flat, palm up, and points their right index finger down into their neighbor's left palm
- On "1, 2, 3, Gotcha!" everyone tries to catch the finger in their left hand while pulling their right finger away to avoid being caught
- Repeat 3–4 rounds with increasing speed

Why We Love It

- **The magic moment:** People inevitably move on "3" before you say "Gotcha," which creates instant hilarity and easy bonds
- **Playfully tests reflexes:** The speed element adds competition without pressure
- **Quick energy shift:** Gets scattered groups focused in minutes

---

Virtual Adaptation: Skip this for virtual teams—it doesn't translate well. Instead, try Rock-Paper-Scissors Showdown or Would You Rather.

Commonalities . . . with Interests!

Time: 8–12 minutes | **Group Size:** Any | **Materials:** None

This takes the basic commonalities concept and adds a crucial restriction that makes it more impactful.

We had a group where the CFO and a new hire discovered they'd both been to the same obscure music festival several times in the 1990s. Six months later, they were regularly going for lunch together. That's what happens when you move past job titles!

How to Play

1. Form small groups (pairs or trios work best)
2. Find 3–5 things you have in common—no work, company, or event talk allowed (otherwise people default to these)
3. Share the most surprising commonality with the full group

Sample prompts:
- "What was your first concert?"
- "What's something you collected as a kid?"
- "What's a skill you wish you had?"

Why We Love It

- ◆ **Prompts authentic connection:** The restriction prevents boring professional commonalities and asks for genuine exploration
- ◆ **Creates lasting inside jokes:** Discoveries become ongoing conversation topics
- ◆ **Works across all personality types:** Introverts and extroverts engage equally

---

Virtual Adaptation: This one is great for breakout rooms (2–3 people per room). At the end, ask each group to share their most surprising discovery.

Would You Rather

Time: 5–10 minutes | **Group Size:** Any | **Materials:** Pre-prepared questions

This classic game offers genuine value for teams when it's structured to reveal values and personality.

The question doesn't matter as much as watching how people think through their answer. I've seen teams learn more about each other in 10 minutes with this than they had in months of meetings.

How to Play

1. Break into groups of 3–5 people
2. Give each group 5–7 questions to discuss
3. Focus on the reasoning behind choices and the conversations around them
4. **Advanced twist:** After discussing, have group members guess what each person didn't choose. This requires active listening and develops an understanding of teammates' preferences.

Sample questions:
- ◆ Would you rather have dinner with your favorite celebrity or travel anywhere for free?

- Would you rather only be able to whisper or only be able to shout?
- Would you rather never have to sleep or never have to eat?

Why We Love It

- **Reveals priorities and values:** You learn more from reasoning than choices
- **Creates lighthearted debate:** It's a low-pressure way to see how people think and their sense of humor
- **Safe vulnerability:** Easier than directly sharing personal information

---

Virtual Adaptation: Perfect choice for breakout rooms. It also works in chat—just post a question, have people respond, and then discuss.

Teach Me!
Time: 10–15 minutes | **Group Size:** Any | **Materials:** None

This one brings out laughs and hidden talents in just a few minutes! It's all about celebrating the weird and wonderful. Plus, there's something so satisfying about sharing expertise, even about silly things.

There's always someone who teaches a fun magic trick or how to moonwalk, and suddenly that quiet person is the coolest person in the room. Everyone gets their minute to shine, and that short time is what creates the humor!

How to Play

1. Explain that each participant gets one minute to "teach" something they're good at
2. Put all the participants' names in a hat and draw names to determine the order

3. When a participant's name is drawn, they'll stand up and teach the group on a 1-minute timer
4. Celebrate the quirky, interesting, and imperfect teaching at the end (and throughout the event)

Why We Love It

- ◆ **Reveals hidden dimensions:** People discover unexpected talents in colleagues
- ◆ **Builds confidence:** Everyone gets to be the expert for a moment
- ◆ **Creates appreciation:** Teams see the diverse capabilities within their group
- ◆ **Generates laughter:** The 1-minute constraint leads to hilarious abbreviated lessons

Virtual Adaptation: This one works beautifully on video calls. Screen sharing and gallery view can enhance demonstrations, enable people to show off things like apps, games, or art skills, and encourage participation.

The Machine
Time: 8–12 minutes | **Group Size:** Any | **Materials:** None

The collaborative nature of this one gives people permission to be weird together. I love watching the first person commit, and then everyone else follows.

By the end, you'll see these people who present themselves as serious professionals being goofy and making robot noises. There are few things as beautiful as giving people permission to be playful.

How to Play

1. Explain that the group will build a human machine with everyone contributing a repetitive motion and sound
2. One volunteer starts in the center with their motion and sound (like a windshield wiper going "whoosh-whoosh" or a robotic arm going "clank-clank")

3. Others join one by one, each adding their own motion and sound that connects to the growing machine, while earlier participants keep going simultaneously
4. Once the whole machine is running, use an imaginary remote to speed it up, slow it down, or make it break down
5. End with applause for the wonderfully weird machine they created—invite people to name it for extra fun

Why We Love It

◆ **Progressive building:** Each person builds on what's already there, with no pressure to be brilliant from scratch
◆ **No right or wrong:** As long as a person adds a sound, they can't "mess up"
◆ **Physical engagement:** Gets people moving and energized
◆ **Group interdependence:** The machine only works if everyone coordinates

---

Virtual Adaptation: This is surprisingly effective virtually! Everyone in the active group unmutes so they can do their sound and motion on camera simultaneously. It's chaotic and delightful. You can also use camera effects (slow motion, speed up) to make it even more engaging.

Snowball
Time: 10–15 minutes | **Group Size:** Any | **Materials:** Paper, pens

This works as both an opener and closer, and it's great for newly-merged or guarded teams.

The anonymous part is fantastic because people write things they'd never say out loud, but once it's on paper and tossed around, suddenly it's safe to talk about. It can break through walls with the most guarded teams.

How to Play

1. Everyone writes three things on paper:
   - One thing they love about their company/team
   - One skill they bring to the group
   - One fun fact about themselves
2. Have everyone crumple papers into "snowballs" and toss them around for 10–15 seconds
3. Call "freeze!" and everyone grabs the nearest snowball
4. **Optional:** Have each person find the author of their snowball, discuss, and then share one new thing they learned about that person

Why We Love It

- **Anonymous sharing:** Reduces pressure and self-consciousness
- **Movement component:** Physical tossing adds energy and playfulness
- **Discovery element:** Finding the author creates natural conversation opportunities
- **Positive focus:** All three prompts highlight strengths and appreciation

> **Virtual Adaptation:** Use a platform that allows anonymous submissions (e.g., Google Forms) and split into breakout rooms if you have a large group. Distribute each group's responses anonymously and let participants try to figure out whose snowball they have in chat.

In the Circle
Time: 8–10 minutes | **Group Size:** 10–50 | **Materials:** None

This one combines high-energy, high-movement, and high-connection moments. It's perfect when energy is flagging or people need to get out of their heads.

When 15 people suddenly run across the circle because they're all afraid of spiders, you can see the connections forming in real time. It's visible proof that we're not as different as we think.

How to Play

1. Everyone stands in a large circle with room to run across
2. One person steps into the center, says their name, and shares one fact about themselves (for example, "I love spicy food!")
3. Anyone who relates to that fact moves to the opposite side of the circle
4. The last person through becomes the next person in the center. Keep going until everyone's had a turn!

Pro Tip: Be mindful of those who may not be able to physically run or move as quickly; change the rules for everyone, or skip this game so no one feels left out.

Why We Love It

◆ **Reminds everyone how similar they are:** Visible connections build fast trust
◆ **Gets people moving:** Breaks people out of sitting and thinking mode
◆ **Chaos is the point:** The energy of running across creates laughter and looseness

Virtual Adaptation: Skip this for virtual teams. The movement element is essential to the experience. Use Commonalities or Would You Rather for remote teams instead.

Group Clap Challenge
Time: 5–10 minutes | **Group Size:** Any | **Materials:** None

This coordination challenge creates genuinely satisfying moments when the group nails it; this typically gets everyone to celebrate together.

Before the eruption of celebration, it's almost meditative when you really get the rhythm synchronized. That relaxed vibe and the feeling of "we did it together" carry over into everything else they do that day.

How to Play

1. **Teach everyone the basic rhythm:** Clap, pause, clap-clap (practice until comfortable)
2. **Add the hand positioning:** Right hand down, left hand up, matching palms with neighbors on both sides
3. **Try the rhythm:** Everyone claps with their neighbors in this position until it's smooth and synchronized
4. **Challenge them:** Reverse hand positions (left down, right up) and maintain the rhythm
5. **Final level:** See if they can switch positions mid-pattern without losing rhythm

Why We Love It

- **Requires genuine coordination:** Teams must work together, watch each other, and adjust timing
- **Creates collective achievement:** That "YES!" moment when it clicks feels amazing
- **Adjustable difficulty:** You can make this easier or harder with new rhythms
- **Focuses scattered groups:** Requires concentration that brings people together

---

Virtual Adaptation: This one works well virtually with some changes. You can either mute your video call and everyone claps together visually or, if your group loves chaos, leave the audio on and have everyone try to sync up with the lag time.

Human Energy Wave

Time: 3–5 minutes | **Group Size:** Any | **Materials:** None

This one captures the collective energy of doing the wave at sporting events in a contained space. It's my go-to when a room feels flat.

In just three minutes, you'll have everyone laughing and energized; it's like hitting a reset button on the whole group.

How to Play

- Pick a "starter" and teach them the countdown: "3, 2, 1, GO!"
- Start the wave with the first row/section standing up, throwing their hands up, and shouting
- Move section by section, building momentum and energy toward the center
- Make the finale explosive with everyone jumping and cheering together

Why We Love It

- **Instant energy:** Deploy when group energy is low
- **Creates collective momentum:** Everyone contributes to something bigger
- **Works as a transition:** Shifts from serious discussion to creative brainstorming
- **Celebration tool:** Marks achievements or milestones with group expression

---

Virtual Adaptation: Believe it or not, this works great on video calls! Use gallery view with everyone unmuted and doing the wave in sequence.

Icebreaker Alert

Time: 10–15 minutes | **Group Size:** 10–50 | **Materials:** Letter cards (one vowel and one consonant per person)

This creative challenge combines individual contribution with group collaboration through word-building.

The negotiation is where the magic happens. Watching people convince others to help make their word or figure out how to merge groups teaches genuine collaboration in real time.

How to Play

1. Give each person a card with one vowel and one consonant
2. People mingle to form small groups and make 2–3 letter words with their combined letters
3. Once someone joins a word group, they're locked in—that group stays together
4. Challenge groups to combine with other groups to create longer words (all members stay together)
5. **Advanced version:** Groups physically arrange themselves crossword-style, connecting their words with other groups

Why We Love It

- ◆ **Creative problem-solving:** Multiple possible solutions for any set of letters
- ◆ **Negotiation skills:** Groups must agree on words and arrangements
- ◆ **Resource management:** Limited letters force strategic thinking

---

Virtual Adaptation: Use shared documents that let people contribute their letters so groups can work together to build words digitally. Use breakout rooms for smaller groups, then bring everyone back to compare.

Notes

Chapter 1

1. https://pmc.ncbi.nlm.nih.gov/articles/PMC3574776/
2. https://files.eric.ed.gov/fulltext/EJ985547.pdf
3. https://par.nsf.gov/servlets/purl/10429504
4. https://www.vedantu.com/blog/how-many-times-edison-failed-to-invent-bulb
5. https://adaa.org/workplace-stress-anxiety-disorders-survey
6. https://www.law.ac.uk/about/press-releases/new-research-communication-crisis/

Chapter 2

1. https://pubmed.ncbi.nlm.nih.gov/30477199/
2. https://www.ragan.com/how-psychological-safety-affects-employee-productivity/
3. Heifetz, R.A., Linsky, M., and Grashow, A. (2009). *The practice of adaptive leadership: Tools and tactics for changing your organization and the world*. Harvard Business Press.
4. https://www.mckinsey.com/featured-insights/diversity-and-inclusion/diversity-wins-how-inclusion-matters
5. https://www.teambonding.com/podcast/diversity-equity-inclusion/
6. https://www.glassdoor.com/blog/6-hr-recruiting-stats-you-need-to-know-for-2018-and-beyond/
7. https://www.ey.com/en_gl/newsroom/2023/09/ey-survey-finds-global-workers-feel-sense-of-belonging-at-their-workplaces-yet-most-are-uncomfortable-sharing-all-aspects-of-their-identities
8. https://www.niagarainstitute.com/blog/emotional-intelligence-statistics
9. https://online.uwa.edu/news/emotional-psychology/

10. https://pmc.ncbi.nlm.nih.gov/articles/PMC9075672/
11. https://greatergood.berkeley.edu/article/item/how_oxytocin_can_make_your_job_more_meaningful
12. https://pmc.ncbi.nlm.nih.gov/articles/PMC6333779/
13. https://pmc.ncbi.nlm.nih.gov/articles/PMC8362988/
14. https://stars.library.ucf.edu/cgi/viewcontent.cgi?article=2673andcontext=etd2020
15. https://alleninstitute.org/news/why-is-the-human-brain-so-difficult-to-understand-we-asked-4-neuroscientists/
16. https://caps.unc.edu/self-help/understanding-mental-health-triggers/

Chapter 3

1. https://www.naceweb.org/about-us/press/despite-overall-dip-in-intern-hiring-more-than-70-percent-of-organizations-plan-to-increase-or-maintain-intern-hiring-levels
2. https://www.gallup.com/workplace/650174/employee-retention-depends-getting-recognition-right.aspx

Chapter 5

1. https://pubmed.ncbi.nlm.nih.gov/33234872/

Chapter 6

1. https://pmc.ncbi.nlm.nih.gov/articles/PMC9053316/

Chapter 7

1. https://pmc.ncbi.nlm.nih.gov/articles/PMC5035282/

Chapter 11

1. https://www.gallup.com/471521/indicator-organizational-culture.aspx

Acknowledgments

This book exists because of the countless people who've walked beside me, believed in me, challenged me, and cheered me on over the years. I've been lucky enough to spend my life in an industry built on connection, and none of this would have been possible without the remarkable individuals and teams who helped bring those connections to life.

First, to Wendy—my partner in every sense of the word. Thank you for your unwavering support, your patience, your honesty, and the way you've always grounded me while still letting me dream big. To Sam, Baylee, and Ty—my greatest joys and my favorite collaborators. You've shaped my world with your humor, your curiosity, and your belief that anything is possible if you just start building it.

To the TeamBonding family—past, present, and future—thank you for your energy, creativity, and dedication to making experiences that matter. You've taken every wild idea and made it better. And to our Catalyst Global partners around the world—thank you for proving that collaboration and connection truly have no borders.

To the early believers: the Mystery Café crew, the Learning Adventure colleagues, and those who said "Yes, let's try it" long before team building was an industry. You took chances with me that changed everything. And to my mother, Bunnie Goldstein—the original family entrepreneur whose Nursery in the Pines planted the seed for everything I would one day build—thank you for showing me what imagination, courage, and a little hustle can create.

A special thank-you to the people I interviewed for this book—Tyler Hayden, Julia Holladay, Paul Giroux, Rob Fletcher, Shannon Lane Dupont, and Jayne Hannah—for sharing your wisdom, stories, and honesty. Your voices added depth and heart to these pages. To my amazing assistant, Lara Campagnolle, thank you for keeping me organized, on track, and sane throughout this entire process. And to Shelby Golding, whose steady guidance and thoughtful wordcraft helped bring these ideas to life—thank you for helping me say what I meant, even when I wasn't sure how to say it.

To my friends and extended family, thank you for helping me stay grounded, inspired, and endlessly entertained. Every conversation, every story, and every shared moment has found its way into the spirit of this book.

And finally, to the thousands of teams who trusted me and my companies over the decades—thank you for letting us play a small part in your journey. Your willingness to show up, dive in, and connect with one another is what keeps me in love with this work.

I'm deeply grateful to every person who helped turn this book from an idea into reality. It took a village, and I couldn't have asked for a better one.

About the Author

David Goldstein has spent nearly four decades doing what he loves most—bringing people together through experiences that make work feel a little more human. As the Founder and Creator of Opportunities at TeamBonding, he has built the leading team building and training company in the United States, earning seven appearances on the Inc. 5,000 list along the way. From global collaborations with Catalyst Global to hands-on events for organizations of every size, David continues to champion the power of play as a serious tool for connection and performance.

His entrepreneurial journey began in 1988 with Mystery Café, the first murder mystery dinner theater in North America, and grew into a collection of creative ventures including Learning Adventure, Recipe for Success, Head First Events, and the Boston Chocolate Tours—his self-described "passion business." A graduate of Emerson College, he lives by the principle that authentic bonds—like those formed through play—create teams that are more collaborative, caring, and effective.

Index